FENG SHUI

THE PILLARS OF DESTINY

RAYMOND LO

TIMES BOOKS INTERNATIONAL
Singapore • Kuala Lumpur

© **1994 Times Editions Pte Ltd**
Reprinted 1996, 1997, 1998

Published by Times Books International
an imprint of Times Editions Pte Ltd
Times Centre
1 New Industrial Road
Singapore 536196
Fax: (65) 2854871 Tel: (65) 2848844
E-mail: te@corp.tpl.com.sg
Online Book Store: http://www.timesone.com.sg/te

Times Subang
Lot 46, Subang Hi-Tech Industrial Park
Batu Tiga
40000 Shah Alam
Selangor Darul Ehsan
Malaysia
Fax & Tel: (603) 7363517
E-mail: cchong@tpg.com.my

Printed by Times Offset (M) Sdn Bhd, Malaysia

ISBN 981 204 480 9

Acknowledgements

I would like to acknowledge the special help of Mr Sara for contributing his fantastic illustrations to this book. My sincere thanks also go to Mr Suen Tai Chuen who, with his enlightened and logical approach, first taught me to decode the secret of Chinese metaphysics. To my wife Maureen, thank you for your continual encouragement and support throughout the preparation of this work.

Contents

Preface

My interest in the occult sciences first began with astrology. Even as a young boy I was fascinated by the accurate description of personality offered by the zodiac signs. The more I used the technique to observe people around me, the more I was convinced that there must be a close connection between man and the cosmos. This stimulated my desire to explore deeper into the mysteries of life and look for a more accurate system of predicting destiny.

As I grew older and began to appreciate oriental culture, I was immediately attracted by the vast treasure of Chinese metaphysics. The major metaphysical texts of the ancient Chinese had, on the orders of an intelligent Emperor of the Ching Dynasty, been included in the compilation of a set of Imperial books called *The Four Libraries of Complete Works*. The section covering metaphysics included nine huge volumes which discussed cosmology, theories about the universe, time and space, human destiny, oracles and *feng shui*. I discovered that some of these theories are so unique to the Chinese that there is often no parallel in other cultures.

Amongst the many subjects covered in these works, it is perhaps *feng shui* and the Four Pillars of Destiny which have the greatest practical relevance to our daily lives. *Feng shui* tells us about the natural forces in our environment and how they affect our well-being, while the art of the Four Pillars of Destiny is a useful tool enabling us to understand our lives and predict our future fortunes. After learning the theory and techniques behind these arts from good masters, I began to put them into practice. Consequently, for many years now I have been fully convinced of the existence of a destiny pattern, revealed through our birth data and the ancient techniques of *feng shui*.

This book is the result of my urge to share such valuable knowledge, especially with English readers who do not have access to the ancient Chinese texts dealing with these subjects. However, to learn and master *feng shui* and the Four Pillars of Destiny is not easy, while explaining them in a language other than Chinese is even more of a challenge. From past experience I have found "logic" to be the key to presenting such techniques to English readers. Therefore, the emphasis of this book is "logical deduction". In each of its two parts, readers will find a short introductory chapter explaining the fundamental theories behind *feng shui* and the Four Pillars, while the following chapters use practical, real-life examples to show the application of these basic theories. Readers may be surprised that the process of analysis used to predict the complicated pattern of life and the impact of our environment is actually made on the basis of a few simple and rational theories. The rest is logical thinking and common sense.

As I intended this book to be current and topical, it offers many recent events, famous buildings and contemporary people as examples with which to demonstrate and verify the techniques of the two philosophies. Much of its contents has also been released to the public in the *feng shui* column of the *Hong Kong Standard* and other media publications between 1990 and 1992. As such, however, the articles were offered as forecasts and predictions about major events. Therefore, this book can be regarded as a form of research into the techniques of Chinese fortune-telling, with the subsequent accuracy of the forecasts providing verification of their validity.

As this book aims to teach practical methods for unveiling the mysteries of life and nature, it is not intended merely for leisure reading. To achieve a better understanding of the process of analysis, the early chapters need to be read carefully and be fully understood before moving on. Many of the techniques introduced here were only available to very few privileged scholars in the past and have never been fully explained in layman's terms, even in Chinese books. Thus, any extra effort spent in understanding the initial theoretical chapters would be very rewarding later on. Finally, *Feng Shui: The Pillars of Destiny* presents an alternative view of life and nature. Whether this is positive or negative is the subject of philosophy and sociology. However, it does present readers with another field of knowledge and I believe the pursuit of knowledge is a positive purpose in life.

PART 1

What is Flying Star Feng Shui?

The term *feng shui* is believed to have first appeared in the ancient Chinese book called *The Rules for Burial*. This text, whilst discussing the influence of energy on the landscape, explains that "the flow of energy dissipated by *wind* stops at the boundary of *water*". Hence, the words *feng shui* literally mean "wind" and "water" respectively. The "energy" mentioned in the text is not clear in meaning, but it is generally believed that it refers to certain abstract natural forces which run with the lie of the landscape and also cast effect on people. This energy has become known as a *feng shui* force.

In simple terms, then, the subject of *feng shui* may be described as one which studies the influence of the environment on human life. However, as its emphasis falls on the analysis of fortune and destiny, it is clearly differentiated from other kinds of social or economic studies of the environment. As *feng shui* forces are natural to the landscape and are believed to cast positive and negative effects on our destinies, the object of the art of *feng shui* is therefore to find ways of making use of the good influences in our environment and avoiding the bad.

Feng shui has a deep-rooted tradition in Chinese culture and there is much in Chinese history that reflects its importance. For instance, most of the palaces and important buildings in China were constructed according to *feng shui* rules, in particular the famous Forbidden City in Beijing which was built to lie exactly on the north-south line. All its constructions, including bridges, stairs, entrances and decorations, were designed according to *feng shui* principles. Besides applying the art in the construction of palaces, the Chinese also believed that burying their ancestors in a good *feng shui* grave site, or *yin* house, would bring prosperity to the descendants of the deceased. Even today, they may still employ a *feng shui* master to find a suitable site. This is often a spot referred to as a "dragon's den", a place where the natural and beneficial *feng shui* forces of a mountain concentrate.

Certain events in Chinese history also reflect the importance of *feng shui*. For example, the Tang Emperors were such firm believers in *feng shui* that they even asked a monk to produce a false *feng shui* book, with the intention of using it to fool their barbarian enemies and bring misfortune upon them. Another interesting example occurred during the Tai Ping Rebellion in the Ching Dynasty, when the Imperial general found the grave site of an ancestor of the rebellion leaders and bombarded it with cannon balls, believing that this would destroy the "dragon's vein" (the beneficial influence of the site) and bring misfortune to the rebels. Indeed, the rebellion was eventually suppressed.

Even now, in the daily life of the Chinese, *feng shui* tradition is still strong. It is common, for instance, to see people put up small hexagonal mirrors outside their windows in the hope of reflecting bad *feng shui*. Many also use an ancient Chinese almanac called the *Tung Sing* which is found to be accurate in predicting the weather. At the same time, however, people still entertain several misconceptions about *feng shui* belief. A common example is the Cantonese aversion to the number four, which sounds like the word "dead" in their dialect. Similarly, many do not like the colour blue because it is used for Chinese funeral lanterns. Both these superstitions are misguided and, as we shall see later in this book, *feng shui* theory actually assigns very different meanings to both the colour and number. However, before correcting these misconceptions and going into detail about *feng shui* symbolism in our daily lives, it is first necessary to have a basic understanding of the fundamental theories from which the subject stems.

Firstly, the *feng shui* environment falls into two categories. One is physical and refers to the visible and tangible features of our surroundings. These include mountains, rivers, buildings, roads, the interior design and layout of houses, and even minor objects of decoration.

Fig. 1 The Tai Chi showing yin and yang

Each item is believed to cast some kind of *feng shui* influence on us. The second type of environment is created by more mysterious and abstract "directional" influences which are invisible, but affect human fortune according to place and time. When evaluating *feng shui* influences, it is absolutely necessary to take both types of environment into consideration. For example, if we consider Chinese palaces like the Forbidden City, we may notice that they were traditionally built with red walls and roofs with sharp edges. In *feng shui* theory, red is regarded as the colour of fire and sharp pointed objects are believed to reflect the shape of fire. Thus the physical appearance of such buildings clearly reflects an image of fire which would surely make them susceptible to destruction by that element. However, it is obvious that not all Chinese palaces have, or will be, burnt down. The reason is that the physical shape alone, without interacting with any intangible directional influence, cannot cause a fire to occur. A fire can only start when stimulated by the arrival of certain directional influences associated with the fire element. Historical records of the Forbidden City tell that a number of fire disasters occurred inside its walls. Each time, however, the city was found to be under the influence of the fire element present in directional forces.

But what exactly are these directional forces? There is a good deal of speculation. Some say they are magnetic waves, while others associate them with cosmic rays and energy. While there has not been any organised scientific study to ascertain their true nature, ancient Chinese scholars apparently discovered a pattern with which to trace their influence and predict their movements. From here they developed theories governing the use and control of these mysterious forces. How they acquired such knowledge is a mystery, although it is believed to have emerged out of a solid foundation in Chinese metaphysical views of the universe and nature. It would be over-ambitious to try to fully explain the whole body of this metaphysical system, but it is possible to give a brief outline of the major theories behind the dynamic *feng shui* philosophy.

As the study of *feng shui* concerns the effects of nature and the environment on human fortune, a complete theory of *feng shui* must comprise at least three aspects: an understanding of nature or the universe, a concept of time and a concept of space.

The Concept of the Universe and Nature

The ancient Chinese people based their theories about nature on the dualism of *yin* and *yang*. They believed that everything possessed a positive male bright side, called the *yang*, but at the same time had a negative female dark side, known as *yin*. These aspects are complementary and integrate with each other, and it is believed that harmony can only be achieved with a balance between the two. This is clearly reflected in the *Tai Chi* diagram (Fig. 1) showing the black and white sides of a circle merging into each other. Such a philosophy is fundamental to Chinese culture.

The next essential theory of nature is that of the five basic elements. This hinges on the belief that everything in the universe is composed of and controlled by five basic forces or kinds of energy. These are symbolised by the five kinds of matter commonly found on earth, namely metal, wood, water, fire and earth. The ancient metaphysical theory of the elements proposed that all matter, material or abstract (including human beings and their fortunes), could be repre-

Fig. 2 The Cycle of Birth and The Cycle of Destruction

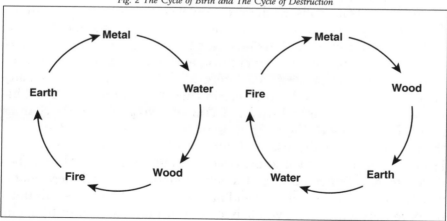

sented by such elements and are subject to their influence. From this belief developed two basic rules which governed the interrelationship between the five elements. These rules are known as "The Cycle of Birth" and "The Cycle of Destruction" (Fig. 2).

The concept of *yin* and *yang* and the two cycles of the five elements are considered the fundamental rules of nature and they appear in all Chinese metaphysical studies. Further explanation of their usage will be found in the discussion of Destiny in the second part of this book.

An explanation of these theories of the universe is not complete without reference to the ancient book called the *I Ching* (*The Book of Change*). It is believed that the theories of *yin* and *yang* and the five elements provide the background to this text, which is regarded by many as a revelation of the ancient people's true understanding of the universe. The author and origin of the book are not clearly known and the original form of it only contains eight linear symbols which we call "trigrams." These are three-line diagrams made up of various combinations of broken and continuous lines. A broken line reflects the *yin* aspect of matter and the continuous line reflects the *yang* aspect. By putting a broken line and continuous line in combinations of three, eight different combinations may be formed and these are called "The Eight Trigrams". Each trigram is assigned a wide variety of meanings, including a basic element, a member of the family, a kind of natural phenomenon, an animal, an organ in the body and even a class of people. In other words, the trigrams are intended to symbolise everything in the universe. By combining any two of these trigrams at random, we obtain a total of sixty-four "hexagrams", each with six lines. These provide more detailed representations of both matter and abstractions, even down to reflecting complicated human relationships. The *I Ching*, as we see it today, is in fact a book consisting of detailed explanations of these sixty-four hexagrams, complied by Confucius and the Emperor of the Chou Dynasty. It can be consulted on all matters and has been used as an oracle among Chinese people for thousands of years.

The Concept of Time

The universe is by no means static and natural influences change with the passage of time. Consequently *feng shui* must also change over time and neither its good nor bad influences can last forever. As such,

15

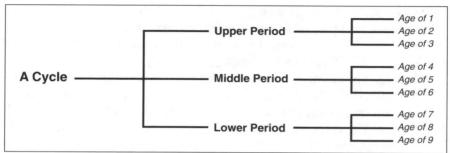

Fig. 3 The Three Periods and Nine Ages

a proper *feng shui* theory must incorporate the element of time and should be able to trace the pattern of change over time.

The *feng shui* system divides time into cycles of 180 years. One such cycle consists of three "Periods" of sixty years, which in turn consists of three "Ages" of twenty years each (see Fig. 3). For example, the twenty-year period from 1984 to 2003 (inclusive) is called the "Age of Seven" and falls under the Lower Period. This concept of age is very significant in the Flying Star method of *feng shui* which I have adopted for this book because, when analysing the *feng shui* of a building or structure, we have to know exactly which Age it was completed in.

The Concept of Space

A firm foundation for a complete *feng shui* theory requires a concept of space. This spatial theory was inspired by a very interesting and mysterious diagram called the *Lo Shu* which was first discovered on the back of a giant tortoise that emerged from the River Lo in central China about 6000 years ago. A reproduction of the original *Lo Shu* diagram is shown in Fig. 4.

This diagram, for convenience sake, is often drawn in the form of a nine square chart with each square representing a direction of the compass. Inside each square we place a number to represent the dots in the original *Lo Shu* diagram (see Fig. 5). This magic nine square chart (also called the *Lo Shu*) forms the foundation for the body of *feng shui* theories generally applied by geomancers today.

The numbers in each square of the *Lo Shu* embrace a variety of meanings. As each represents a trigram of the *I Ching*, all the hidden meanings of the trigrams are incorporated. For instance, each number bears reference to a basic element, a family member, a natural phe-

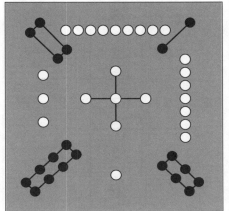

4	9	2
3	5	7
8	1	6

S — N — E — W

Fig. 4 The Lo Shu diagram   Fig. 5 The Lo Shu expressed in numbers

nomenon and possesses both a *yin* and *yang* character (see the table of meanings on page 34). Furthermore, as time is divided into nine Ages of twenty years, every number symbolises an Age. For example, the present Age of Seven (1984 to 2003 inclusive) means that the number 7 is the most prosperous number in our Age, while the number 8 represents prosperity in the immediate future. Any number smaller than 7 symbolises prosperity in the past and will not bring beneficial influences in the present Age. The number 5, however, is also central and regarded as a controlling and balancing power. It does not belong to any trigram so does not carry a wealth of meanings like other numbers. We may additionally note that the arrangement of these numbers in the *Lo Shu* diagram is such that the sum of each line (whether vertical, horizontal or diagonal) always equals fifteen.

I have emphasised to readers that the Flying Star school of *feng shui* is dynamic in the sense that it incorporates the time element. In the same way, the *Lo Shu* diagram, represented by the nine square chart, changes with time. The numbers inside each square are dynamic and move in a fixed pattern. If the centre number is replaced, the other numbers automatically change position around it, according to the following pattern of movement:

Centre	NW	W	NE	S	N	SW	E	SE
5	6	7	8	9	1	2	3	4

Since the numbers of the *Lo Shu* represent a type of *feng shui* influence present in a certain direction, this numerical change consequently reveals to us how the forces of nature change with time in a fixed pattern. The position of the numbers in the diagram thus changes from Age to Age, from year to year, from month to month, even from day to day, according to the pattern shown above. For example, to find the *feng shui* forces present in different directions during the Age of Seven (1984-2003), we put the number 7 in the middle square and place the consecutive numbers 8 and 9 around it. According to the sequence above, if 7 is in the central position, 8 will move to the north-west and 9 to the west, which is followed by 1 in the north-east and so on until the numbers form a new nine square chart as shown in Fig. 6.

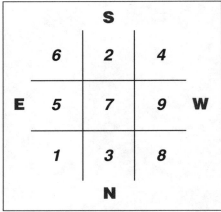

Fig. 6 Feng shui chart for the Age of Seven

It is worth getting familiar with this kind of nine square chart as it is the basis for detecting the *feng shui* influences affecting buildings. Given the age of a building, along with its direction, we can immediately draw up a nine square chart showing the intangible forces affecting it from all directions. This is called the *feng shui* or "flying star" chart of the building. If we take one step further and compare the directional influences of a certain year or month with the flying star chart of the building, we may see how the numbers, or flying stars, interact with one another. It is by such methods that we can assess the fortune of a building and predict happenings within it. This technique of the Flying Star school was a well kept secret in the past. Rediscovered in the Ching Dynasty, it has now become the most popular and practical method used by *feng shui* experts today.

How to Apply Flying Star Feng Shui

In the last chapter, I presented readers with a good deal of the terminology and theory surrounding *feng shui*. Some of this is very abstract and complicated. To achieve a better understanding of the subject I propose to take readers on a field trip and conduct a practical exercise in *feng shui* analysis.

Assuming I receive a request to inspect the *feng shui* of a residential building, the first step before setting out is to collect some background information. The most essential information a *feng shui* expert requires is the age of the building. As I mentioned in the previous chapter, time is divided into Ages of twenty years each. For instance, buildings that were constructed and completed in the period between 1964 and 1983 (inclusive) are called Age of Six buildings and their *feng shui* influence differs totally from a building completed before or after that Age, even though they may be sitting on the same site, facing the same direction. Other information usually required for a field trip is the birth data of the residents of the house. This is used in a number of ways. Firstly, people born in different years receive different *feng shui* influences and it is essential to determine if there is any *feng shui* conflict between the dwellers' birth data and the direction of the house. Secondly, this birth data can assist both in selecting the best colour scheme and decorations for the residents to use, and in choosing their most suitable sleeping locations. In this latter respect, we are in fact dealing with the technique of the Four Pillars of Destiny and more discussion about the usage of birth data will be found in the second part of this book. Besides collecting data about the house, it is also helpful if the client can explain any particular reasons for requesting a *feng shui* analysis so that problem areas may be specifically addressed.

Before taking the field trip, let us carefully examine all the necessary tools. There are not many items for *feng shui* field work, but the most essential and indispensable instrument is the *lo pan*, the Chinese *feng shui* compass (see Fig. 7). To explain in the simplest terms, this is a compass with a magnetic needle for measuring directions. Unlike common compasses, however, it includes numerous concentric rings, each showing complicated trigrams, stars, heavenly stems, earthly branches and numbers. Its complexity may be off-putting, but most of the symbols are in fact only used in selecting grave sites, or *yin* houses.

Fig. 7 The Twenty-four Mountains of the lo pan

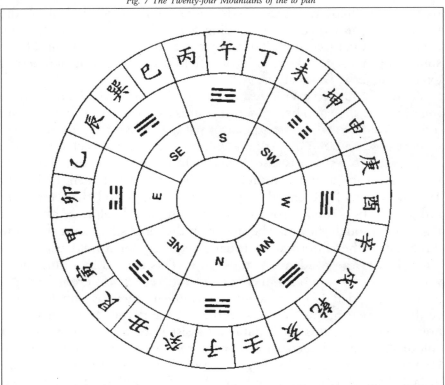

To analyse the *feng shui* of *yang* houses (houses for the living), beginners need only be familiar with the ring known as the "Twenty-four Mountains". This comprises 360 degrees divided into 24 sections, each occupying 15 degrees.

Besides the compass, I usually carry a booklet called *The Thousand Years Almanac*. This is used for converting the Western calendar into Chinese and in measuring the dimensions of a house. I also use another measuring device, usually a sonic ruler, so that floor plans can be drawn to scale.

I emphasised in the last chapter that there are two aspects to *feng shui*, the physical environment and intangible influences. The first step in inspecting the building is to walk around the site to observe its physical surroundings and to establish its directions. The decision about a building's direction is very important as this is an essential step in drawing up its *feng shui* chart. Any error made at this stage could render the entire *feng shui* assessment worthless and misleading. In the old days it was easy to establish the front and back of a building as most constructions were of normal rectangular shape, with the front entrance usually representing the direction of the building. However, modern buildings, especially skyscrapers, often come in very irregular forms and frequently require hair-splitting consideration when determining their front and back. This skill can only be enhanced with more experience and a solid theoretical foundation to assist your judgement.

Having established the direction of a building we can then measure it accurately with the *lo pan* and record the direction bearings. When measuring, it is recommended to stand in an unobstructed open space, as far away from the building as possible. This is because the concrete mass of a huge building or any metal objects nearby will usually affect the magnetic needle of the compass and lead to inaccurate direction readings. For the same reason, I never trust the compass once I have walked inside a building as the readings inside a house are affected by furniture and fixtures. On the basis of the age of the house and its direction readings we may now draw up a *feng shui* chart in the nine square format, showing all the influences the building will receive from all directions. After completing this preparatory work, we are ready to go upstairs to inspect the specific apartment in the block.

On entering the flat, we must ascertain in which part of the building it is located and what its relative direction is. Then we may inspect the entire flat, room by room, to get an idea of its general layout for a floor plan. Fig. 8 is a *feng shui* chart showing the apartment's directional influences, while Fig. 9 shows the corresponding floor plan. The large number 6 in the centre of Fig. 8 shows that this building was constructed in the Age of Six (1964 to 1983 inclusive). The small pairs of numbers in each square show *feng shui* influences commonly called "flying stars". The numbers

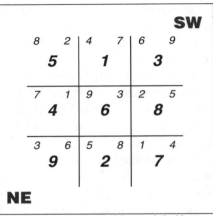

Fig. 8 Feng shui chart of the sample building

on the right are specifically called "mountain stars" and affect human prosperity or health, while the numbers on the left are called "water stars" and govern financial fortune. These numbers move in the same pattern as the *Lo Shu* diagram. In general, one should note that a prosperous water star is best found in a mobile, fluid or active location, such as the front entrance, the living room and the open spaces of a building. On the other hand, the mountain star should fall in a solid, high, enclosed and preferably quiet location, such as the areas occupied by tall buildings and the bedrooms inside a house. This is particularly true for the mountain and water stars represented by the numbers 7 and 8 as, in the present Age of Seven, these numbers represent prosperity in the present (7) and immediate future (8).

Fig. 9 Sample floor plan

With a floor plan of the flat in one hand and the *feng shui* chart of the building in the other, an expert can start making comments about the positive and negative aspects of the whole building, how its surroundings and intangible forces are affecting financial and human prosperity. The same *feng shui* chart may also be applied to describe the prosperity of the flat inside. The essential item to note is the location of the main entrance, as all good or bad influences come through the front door. Equally essential is the location of the master bedroom which very much affects the health and prosperity of the entire household.

The main entrance to the flat in Fig. 9 is in the north-east location. The corresponding *feng shui* chart shows the numbers 3 and 6 in this location. This means that the front entrance of the flat is subject to the influence of the *feng shui* forces represented by these two stars. As the entrance to a home or building is a location of activity, a mobile and fluid place, the major emphasis falls on the water star, which is in this case represented by the number 6. This is not considered a beneficial star and we can therefore infer that the entrance is not favourably located to admit financial prosperity.

A good *feng shui* expert will thoroughly comment on the location of every major room in an apartment, along with the placement of furniture and decorative objects within it. This includes advice on the positioning of beds, desks, cookers, toilets, TV sets and telephones, as well as a detailed explanation of how the floor layout and the position of each object will affect the prosperity of the house. Besides interior decoration, he will also explain how outside surroundings affect the home. All of this information goes hand in hand with his analysis of the birth data of the residents, which judges their compatibility with the house and determines suitable colour schemes and decor.

I have emphasised in several places that *feng shui* reading is dynamic as its influence changes over time. Consequently the *feng shui* master will look some months into the future in order to inform the household what they should be prepared for. For example, if the inauspicious star yellow 5 is expected to arrive in the front entrance of a house during a particular month, the expert will tell the household to hang a wind chime at the front entrance in that month to dissolve the bad influence.

Returning to our example, the chart shown in Fig. 8 only displays the static *feng shui* influence of the building. There are also yearly, monthly and even daily *feng shui* influences which will interact with the static *feng shui* chart of the building to cause and influence events.

23

These yearly, monthly and daily *feng shui* forces, or flying stars, move in the same pattern as the *Lo Shu* diagram discussed in the last chapter and can also be expressed in a nine square chart. Fig. 10 shows such a flying star chart reflecting influences in the month of November 1992. By superimposing this monthly star chart onto the static *feng shui* chart of the building, we can see that the yearly star 2 and monthly star 5 arrived at the north-east location in November 1992. This is the location of the main entrance to the flat. As the star 5 symbolises trouble and the star 2 represents sickness, it is not surprising to discover that the head of the household of this flat was indeed hospitalized in November of that year.

1	6	8
7	**3**	**5**
9	2	4
6	**8**	**1**
5	7	3
2	**4**	**9**

Fig. 10 Flying star chart for November 1992

Before leaving the residence, the *feng shui* expert will give an overall view of the house and make recommendations for measures which should be taken to ward off future threats to prosperity. It is also my practice to make detailed measurements of the house so I can draw up a floor plan to scale. This is essential in reconfirming which section of a house comes under which directional *feng shui* influence. A rough sketch of the floor plan is usually not accurate enough for a detailed interpretation. Finally, a full report must be prepared for the client, recording all comments and explanations, and illustrated with drawings and recommendations. Again I consider this a vital step, for it not only provides the client with clear instructions for necessary changes, but also gives the *feng shui* expert a complete record of previous assignments should the same client have follow-up requests in the future.

Readers should by now possess a general idea of what *feng shui* is and what a *feng shui* expert is expected to do in providing a service. If readers wish to look deeper into the technical aspects of the field and conduct their own experiments, a knowledge of how to draw up *feng shui* charts and interpret the stars will be required. The formulae behind the making of these charts are very complicated but, for convenience, *Appendix 1* at the back of this book shows all the *feng shui* charts for Age of Seven buildings (those completed between 1984 and 2003 inclusive). Readers need only measure the direction of a building and select the applicable chart from the Appendix. The proper interpretation of these charts requires deeper knowledge and experience, and I believe this is best conveyed as I lead you through the real life examples given in the following chapters.

The Flaws in the Hong Kong Legco Building

In 1992 there was considerable controversy surrounding members of the Hong Kong Legislative Council. Since the commencement of the new session in October 1991, one elected member had been convicted of forgery, while another was under investigation for bribery. As the Year of the Monkey began, yet another member was reported to be suffering form a serious illness and had to be hospitalised. With the apparent rise in misfortunes associated with Legco members, people naturally became concerned about the *feng shui* of the old building. *Feng shui* even took the blame for minor personal mishaps, such as the theft of a private car belonging to a member. It would be interesting to examine this controversy from a genuine *feng shui* perspective and see what conclusions ancient theory can draw about these misfortunes.

The Legco Building is situated on a superb site in central Hong Kong, termed a "dragon's den". This is a spot where the energy of the Victoria Mountain concentrates, providing the strongest potential for prosperity. The Hongkong Bank is on the same site and its financial prosperity contributes tremendously to the economy. Nevertheless, a good location is not enough to guarantee good *feng shui*. We must also examine the direction of the building and draw up a chart which shows what *feng shui* influences the building will receive from different directions.

To perform this more technical task, let us look at the history of the building as engraved on a bronze plate in Statue Square. The building was recorded as being constructed between the years 1899 and 1910. It was inaugurated as the Supreme Court on 15 January 1912 and was subsequently converted to the present Legislative Council Building between 1984 and 1985. The direction of the building was measured to be on the east-west line. Equipped with such information, I have drawn up a *feng shui* chart as shown in Fig. 11.

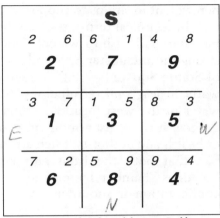

Fig. 11 *Feng shui chart of the Legco Building*

This chart shows the *feng shui* influences the building will receive from all directions. To interpret it in detail is a very technical task and I do not intend to bore readers with *feng shui* jargon. To understand this chapter, readers need only know that the small numbers 7 and 8 found in the east and south-west sectors symbolise prosperity, and that such prosperity came into effect in 1984 and will last until the year 2023. As the rear entrance of the Legco Building faces the Chater Garden and is in the east, it is well-positioned to receive prosperous influences. Perhaps this is the reason why it was converted into the Legco Building during 1984 and 1985.

As we mentioned in the previous chapter, the *feng shui* expert examines the physical surroundings of a building to see whether it is in harmony with mountains and water. Mountains symbolise the human aspects of *feng shui*, while water represents finances. In a modern city, however, we look at tall buildings instead of mountains, and traffic and roads instead of water. To interpret the *feng shui* chart, readers should note that the small numbers on the right in each sector represent the water aspect (water stars) while those on the left denote mountain aspects (mountain stars).

The water aspect of the Legco Building is very good. This means it can be a prosperous building if used for commercial and financial purposes. To the contrary, the mountain configuration is not good. This means the other buildings surrounding the Legco are not in benevolent locations to support its mountain stars (or human prosperity). In technical terms, such configurations are referred to as "mountain stars falling into water". One prominent example of this is the strong mountain star 8, found in the west sector. This is the location of Statue Square (see Fig. 12) which, as an open space, is regarded as water in *feng shui* terminology. So the mountain star has fallen into water in the west location, bringing with it problems of human relevance, such as disharmony in relationships and instability in matters of health and authority. Such adverse effects are also intensified by the fact that both the front entrance of the Legco Building and the Meeting Chamber happen to be located in the west. Perhaps this configuration of "mountain star falling into water" at the west entrance

Fig. 12 The environment of the Hong Kong Legco Building

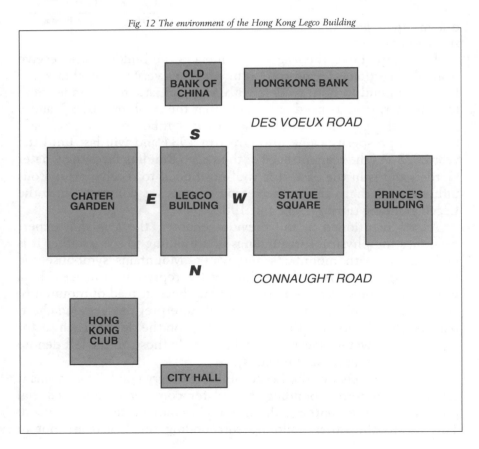

is the greatest cause of human disharmony and the main drawback in the *feng shui* of the building. As the east entrance facing the Chater Garden is more prosperous, it should be used more often, but I understand that the public entrance is still in the west.

The *feng shui* chart of the building, moreover, shows a weak location in the north, symbolised by the small number 5. This number is often taboo in the Flying Star school of *feng shui*. However, it is said that the government officials sit in that direction to debate and address questions. This is certainly not an auspicious spot for such activities.

Inside the Meeting Chamber, the Chairman's seat is located in the east, where the mountain star is represented by a weak number 3 (see Fig. 13). Behind the Chairman's seat is the Chater Garden. The

Fig. 13 Seating arrangement in the Meeting Chamber

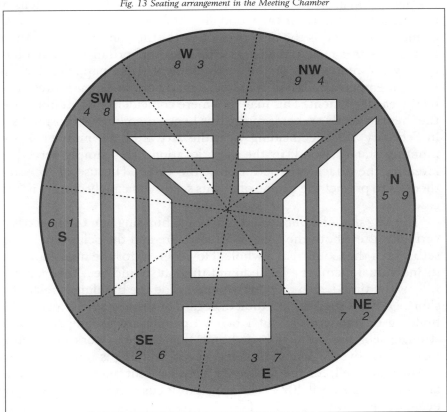

buildings in the east are too far away to provide solid support to the Chairman's position. This is again a sign of weakness in power and authority. Despite the fact that *feng shui* influences are dynamic and change from year to year, it is clear that hard times are still ahead for this building and its members. While in 1992 the *feng shui* at the west entrance indicated an increase in spending and weak human prosperity, in 1993 the unfavourable star yellow 5 moves to the east, precisely where the chairman's seat is located.

I have one further finding which may prove interesting here. *Feng shui* theory can also tell which location is most favourable, or unfavourable, to a person born in a certain year. One Legco member who recently fell ill was actually sitting in an unsuitable spot for his year of birth. His seat is in the west sector of the *feng shui* chart where we see the pair of small numbers, 3 and 8. Advanced *feng shui* theory tells us the number 3 stands for the wood element and 8 stands for the earth element. As wood is the destroyer of earth, the combination of these two elements is most unfavourable to a person born in a year symbolised by the number 8, or the earth element. It so happens that the Legco member who fell ill is indeed a man born in a year represented by the earth element. This may be a mere coincidence but it illustrates the theory exactly. What is more, this Legco member was hospitalised in February 1992, coinciding with the arrival of the number 4, the monthly star of wood, in the west location. This simply served to intensify the attack of wood against the earth. The use of *feng shui* theories to predict the timing of events seems amazingly correct in this case.

The *feng shui* of a public and functional building like the Legco will certainly affect both the general atmosphere and the achievements or setbacks of the Council as a whole. However, as for the misfortunes of its individual members, I still do not think it should bear the blame in full, as the time Legco members spend inside the building is relatively short. I am not suggesting a total disregard of the *feng shui* effect of this building on individuals, but I believe people are usually subject to stronger *feng shui* influences at home than at their work or meeting places. The overall *feng shui* of the Legco Building is not completely negative after all, for the prosperity at its east entrance is expected to last for 40 years until 2023. The apparent focus on the rise in unhappy events may have created a false impression. Legco members now capture much more public attention than in previous years, so any minor occurrence, such as the theft of a car, may be blown up to controversial scale by the media.

Finally, I cannot recommend any method of improvement to the building without more detailed information on its interior arrangement. My only advice would be to avoid the construction or placement of large obstructions in the eastern location as this is a prosperous direction and should remain open and receptive to prosperity.

Unveiling the Secrets of a Casino – The Hotel Lisboa

Amongst the famous buildings in Southeast Asia, the Hotel Lisboa in Macau is perhaps one of the most controversial and interesting. Being a popular casino, there are many rumours surrounding the mysterious nature of the building and most Chinese people believe that its design is totally geared to *feng shui* principles which generate prosperity for its owner, the tycoon Mr Stanley Ho. Indeed, after seriously studying and measuring the building, I cannot help believing that it was designed by the capable hand of a professional *feng shui* master.

The most prominent feature of the Hotel Lisboa is its cylindrical tower, which also houses its main entrance. This tower has the appearance of a bird cage, a symbolic indication that wealth is captured and securely retained in the casino. On the top of the tower, protruding from the roof, there are many unique decorative objects. Some say these are sabres, placed to defend the casino from gamblers entering through the main entrance. However, a more authentic belief is that these objects (sixty-four in number) match the sixty-four hexagrams of the *I Ching* and serve as antennas, receiving prosperity from all directions. Moreover, the ledges surrounding the building are shaped like bats, a traditional symbol of fortune and riches. The entrance is also said to be in the shape of a bat's mouth, wide open and ready to absorb wealth and prosperity.

However, these features are all superficial arrangements and *feng shui* theory can be applied much more deeply to this building. The best *feng shui* technique is the specific employment of the abstract directional forces, or flying stars, to intensify the prosperity of the place. To understand the working of such directional forces on the hotel, its true bearings must first be established.

Evaluating the *feng shui* of such a vast construction as the Hotel Lisboa is not an easy task. To protect its *feng shui* secrets, I also believe some kind of camouflage technique might have been applied in its design. The purpose of such a measure could be to deter gamblers, with the assistance of a *feng shui* master, from finding out its weak areas and causing the casino to lose money. In the past, one common camouflage technique was to build walls around major buildings to conceal their true directions. This seems to have been very skilfully implemented by the designer of the Lisboa, as several *feng shui* students have previously been fooled. In one article discussing the *feng shui* of the building, the author was totally misled by its superficial direction and concluded that the hotel was not built according to Flying Star theory at all.

Such a mistake may have arisen from the fact that many people take the main entrance in the round tower as the front door and measure direction from there. However, I must explain that many modern buildings are constructed with their main entrances facing one direction and the rest of the building facing another. Prominent examples of this are the entrances to the numerous Heng Seng Banks in Hong Kong which usually position their main entrances on the corner of a building, making an angle of about 45 degrees to the street. This is necessary from the *feng shui* point of view to ensure that the entrance faces a prosperous direction. However, such direction only governs the *feng shui* of the main entrance and the other influences received still rely on the direction of the rest of the building.

The Hotel Lisboa has obviously employed this technique in its design: the front door in the round tower is set in the direction SSW, whereas the rest of the building is constructed in the direction SWW. If we make the mistake of taking the direction of the main entrance as that of the whole building, the *feng shui* chart drawn up from such measurements will certainly not reflect a prosperous enterprise like the Hotel Lisboa. That is why some *feng shui* experts simply discard it as not being built according to *feng shui* theory. This mistake only reflects how clever the original designer was in concealing these an-

		S			
1	4	5	8	3	6
	5		**1**		**3**
2	5	9	3	7	1
	4		**6**		**8**
6	9	4	7	8	2
	9		**2**		**7**

Fig. 14 Feng shui chart of the Hotel Lisboa

cient secrets. If one goes round the whole hotel and observes it from all sides, instead of being preoccupied by its grand entrance, it is not so difficult to see the true front and back directions. According to my observations, the building faces SWW and the grand entrance, in fact, only sits on the southern corner of the whole edifice.

On such a hypothesis, one may draw up a *feng shui* chart showing a prosperous entrance at the south, symbolised by the water star 8 (see Fig. 14). The benevolent influence of such a water star is also intensified by the circular nature of a nearby park, a roundabout traffic system, as well as the river flowing right in front of the main entrance in the south. So, with a *feng shui* chart drawn up on the basis of the SWW direction, it seems that every piece of the jigsaw puzzle falls into its proper place. We can see that the building is designed to be totally in tune with Flying Star theories, as the prosperous water star is neatly placed in water to absorb prosperity from all directions.

The chart in Fig. 14 shows that the most prominent water stars, 8 and 7, symbolising financial gains, are situated in the south and north locations. Theoretically, therefore, these locations and entrances will bring the most profit to the casino. By the same token, the less prosperous water stars on the chart show weaker locations where the casino is more susceptible to loss and gamblers stand a bigger chance of winning.

One recent controversy surrounding the Hotel Lisboa concerns the possible effect of the new Bank of China building rising up in the hotel's west location. Many worried that this very tall building, with its two gigantic lion statues, would compete with the casino for the benevolent *feng shui* influences and reduce its prosperity. However, this is clearly not the case if one puts the Bank of China building on the *feng shui* chart above. The tall bank is located in the west sector, where we find the prosperous mountain star 7. It thus acts as a tall mountain and only serves to intensify the power of such a prosperous mountain star. This increases human prosperity and we can expect visitors to the Hotel Lisboa to grow in number, with more people using the lucky west entrance.

I must conclude with a warning that the above chart only shows the static *feng shui* influence of the building. Such an influence must interact with the yearly, monthly and daily flying stars which can bring about complete changes in fortune. While the static chart shows the long term influences, it is not adequate for daily reference. Consequently, gamblers are not recommended to rely on the chart when selecting their gambling places or planning their strategies.

Bad Feng Shui
in a House
of Tragedy

In the first chapter of this book I briefly introduced readers to the interpretation of numbers, a basic technique of the Flying Star school of *feng shui*. The meaning of these numbers originates from the trigrams of the *I Ching*. Each number in fact represents a trigram, but while there are altogether eight basic trigrams, there are nine numbers from 1 to 9. This is because the number 5 does not symbolise a trigram, but is considered a unique number occupying "middle earth" and balancing the interaction between conflicting elements.

For quick reference, the following table summarises the essential meanings attached to each number.

No.	Element	Person	Colour	Object	Body	Trigram
1	Water	Middle-aged man	Black	Blood, Den	Ear	
2	Earth	Old woman	Black	Earth, Ox	Stomach	
3	Wood	Eldest son	Green	Thunder	Foot	
4	Wood	Elder daughter	Green	Wind	Buttocks	
5	Earth	–	Yellow	Misfortune	–	–
6	Metal	Father	White	Heaven	Head	
7	Metal	Young girl	White	Lake	Mouth	
8	Earth	Young son	White	Mountain	Hands	
9	Fire	Middle daughter	Red	Sun, Beauty	Eyes	

This table shows the meaning of single numbers representing a single trigram. However, students of the *I Ching* should note that a combination of two trigrams becomes a *kua* and there are in total 64 *kua*, or pairs of trigrams, in the *I Ching*, each of them being assigned more complex meanings. This gives rise to the fascinating interpretation of pairs of numbers which is unique to Chinese metaphysics and has no parallel in Western numerology.

One trigram, for instance, represents a fixed element or object, but two trigrams, one over the other, bring about interactions between two elements, causing the objects to come alive with dynamic meaning. For example, the trigram ☱ represents the lake and the element of metal, while the trigram ☲ symbolises the element of fire. The two combined form a *kua* called "Revolution". The *I Ching* provides the following explanation of this *kua*:

"The young lady is above and the older lady is below, and what results is essentially only an opposition of tendencies. The influences are in actual conflict and the forces combat each other like fire and water (lake), each trying to destroy the other. Hence the idea of revolution."

Likewise, the trigram ☲ is symbolised by the number 9, while the trigram ☱ is symbolised by the number 7. The coupling of these numbers, 9 and 7, will also bear a similar meaning of conflict and disaster associated with fire.

It is not possible for such an introductory book to list all the meanings of number combinations. However, there are a few essential and interesting pairs which are easy for readers to remember:

1 and 4: water gives birth to wood. This means literature, art, academic achievement or promotion. However, it can also signify romance or a sex scandal when under a bad influence.

4 and 8: the number 8 is by nature the earth element but it also symbolises the young son or child. The number 4 is the element of wood, the destroyer of earth. Consequently, this pair of numbers is not favourable to children.

7 and 3: metal clashes with wood. This pair of numbers signifies robbery, conflict and discord.

9 and 6: this is not a positive pair as fire destroys metal and means a fire disaster. The number 6 also symbolises the father or head of the family, so this pair can also reflect harm to the father.

9 and 8: fire gives birth to earth. This pair usually symbolises happy occasions such as marriages or celebrations. As 8 refers to young children, it can also mean the joy of a new born baby.

2 and 5: sickness is often associated with the number 2, while 5 symbolises misfortune. This pair of numbers should certainly be avoided.

The combination of numbers is not restricted to pairs. They can be expanded to combinations of three or more. For example, the three numbers 7, 9 and 5 can be interpreted as representing heavy smoking or drug addiction as they create the scenario of mouth (7), fire (9) and evil (5). Readers can interpret any combination of numbers at hand, including telephone and car registration numbers, by just applying the theory of the five elements and their basic meanings. Let your imagination fly and you may discover a number of surprises.

The symbolic interpretation of the nine numbers has often been employed by *feng shui* experts of the Flying Star school to predict and describe domestic events. In the essential *feng shui* classics written by Master Sum of the Ching Dynasty, a number of examples are included to display how numbers can vividly describe murder scenes, supernatural occurrences and suicides. To help readers understand this amazing technique, I am going to apply the theory of numerical interpretation to a tragedy which recently made headline news in Hong Kong.

On 7 May 1990, the bodies of a family of five, including the parents and three young children, were found lying unconscious in an apartment in Kowloon. The father and three children were certified dead and the mother was subsequently put on trial for manslaughter. The incident was extensively covered by the Hong Kong press and the general public was shocked by the apparent senselessness of the killings.

When applying *feng shui* theory to this case, we must remember that family conflict involves complicated human relationships which often generate deep emotions. Whether this conflict will end in a quarrel or be resolved peacefully is determined by individual fortunes and self control, not only the environmental influences of *feng shui*. The lack of availability of the victim's birth data precludes any detailed fortune analysis. However, I have taken some measurements of the *feng shui* surrounding the flat and, on the basis of sketches of the death scene which appeared in the press, I am able to offer some explanations.

The death flat is a unit in an Age of Six building with its front door facing the north-east and its back against the south-west. Fig. 15 shows the approximate location of the flat in the building, along with its physical surroundings, while the *feng shui* chart of such a house is shown in Fig. 16. The nine square chart of the flat shows the distribution of the intangible *feng shui* influences, represented by the small numbers in the eight directions. Being a house built in the Age of Six, we shall first see whether the various placements of the number 6 (meaning prosperity in the Age of Six) are properly located.

From the chart, readers can see that the mountain star 6 (the small number on the left of a square) is located in the south-west at the back of the house, whereas the water star 6 (the small number on the right) is located in the north-east, the front of the house. The first law of Flying Star *feng shui* is that the prosperous water star should be positioned in water and the prosperous mountain star located on the mountain. Let us compare Fig. 15 and Fig. 16 to see whether the physical circumstances of the flat match with this principle.

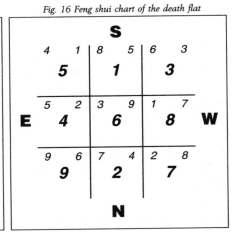

Fig. 15 Environment of the death flat   Fig. 16 Feng shui chart of the death flat

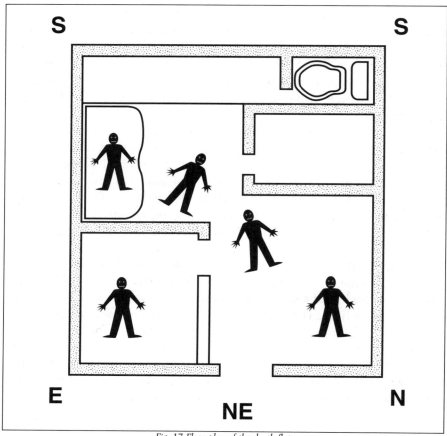

Fig. 17 Floor plan of the death flat

The sketch shows that there is open space both at the front and at the back of the flat. This configuration means that the residence may enjoy prosperity in terms of wealth, as the water star 6 is located at the front door. However, it is not so fortunate in terms of its human aspects, such as health and relationships, as the mountain star 6 at the back falls into open space. This is termed a "mountain star falling into water" and is a serious drawback to human harmony.

As the art of *feng shui* is closely related to individual birth data, its impact on people varies. People born in different years are assigned different *kua*, which can also be represented by a number. This personal *kua* is often an essential factor in deciding which member of the family will bear the brunt of bad *feng shui*. For example, if the flying star 6 is poorly located in a residence, the person who is born in the year when the *kua* is represented by 6 will suffer most.

In the case of the death flat in Kowloon, it was reported that the principle victim, the father, was aged 50. A man born in the year 1940 is a person of the *kua* symbolised by the number 6. Consequently, the mountain star 6 falling into water is likely to cast a bad influence on him. Furthermore, the front door of the flat is located in the north-east, where we find the two small numbers, 9 and 6. Readers can see from the table in this chapter that 9 is a female number and belongs to the fire element, whereas 6 means the father and belongs to the metal element. As fire destroys metal, the configuration of 9 and 6 appearing at the front door obviously suggests that the father will encounter misfortune, particularly as he was born under the *kua* of 6. Conflict and misfortune involving the paternal head of the family is, in this case, literally written on the front door.

Let us also examine the interior arrangement of the flat from the *feng shui* perspective and analyse the impact of negative intangible forces that concentrated there on 7th May 1990.

Fig. 17 is a sketch which appeared in newspapers and shows the interior layout of the flat and the death scene. The essential location, besides the front entrance, is the master bedroom where the father's body was found. This room is located in the east. Comparing its location with the *feng shui* chart in Fig. 16, we can see the two unlucky numbers 5 and 2, representing misfortune, are concentrated in the same east location. Thus the bedroom is poorly located and will certainly bring misfortune to people sleeping there.

The next area to examine is the west location, where we find a prosperous water star 7. If this star can be properly activated, it will bring financial gains to the household. Unfortunately we can see that the west of the flat is the location of the kitchen and toilet. The prosperous star 7 belongs to the metal element but the kitchen and stove are symbols of fire. Thus it will not enhance prosperity at all, since fire destroys metal. Moreover, as the toilet is an outlet of water, placing a prosperous water star there is equivalent to literally flushing prosperity away.

Besides the main entrance, another major inlet of *feng shui* influence is the corridor, which is situated in the south and south-west

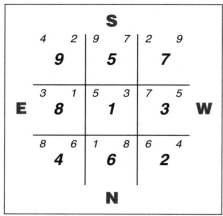

S

| 4 2 | 9 7 | 2 9 |
| **9** | **5** | **7** |

| 3 1 | 5 3 | 7 5 |
| **E** **8** | **1** | **3** **W** |

| 8 6 | 1 8 | 6 4 |
| **4** | **6** | **2** |

N

Fig. 18 Flying star chart for 7th May 1990

locations. Turning to the *feng shui* chart, we find that the water stars in these two squares are 5 and 3. Both are unfavourable stars and will not be supportive of any prosperity in the house. With so many material drawbacks, we can now be sure that the *feng shui* configuration for the house of the tragedy is very poor. The danger of ill fortune is already ominous and it only takes a yearly or monthly star to arrive at the essential spots to trigger some unhappy event.

Now let us examine the *feng shui* stars on the date of the tragedy. Fig. 18 shows the position of flying stars on the date. In the centre square the large number is the yearly star for 1990, the small number on the left is the monthly star for May and the one on the right is the daily star for 7th May. Let us see how these clusters of stars affect the house on that date. First we must consider the important western location, as this is both the position of the flat in the building and the location of the entrance to the master bedroom. The chart shows a concentration of the stars 7, 3, and 5 here. As 7 is metal and 3 is wood, these two stars are in conflict and reflect arguments and discord. The star 5 additionally spells trouble and the general picture is of misfortune arising from quarrels.

Another major spot to examine is the north-east, which is the location of the main entrance. Here the chart shows the presence of the numbers 4 and 6. As the number 4 represents a girl and romance, and the number 6 symbolises the father, this combination offers a picture of some kind of romantic scandal involving the father. Besides the main entrance, the corridor in the south location shows a concentration of 5, 7 and 9. This conflicting configuration of metal and fire, coupled with the ominous star 5, only adds intensity to the misfortune. Earlier in this chapter I indicated that the combination of numbers 5, 7 and 9 can refer to oral poisoning, such as heavy smoking or drug addiction, since they are symbolic of evil, the mouth and fire respectively. Considering the prominence of this configuration in the death flat, it thus corresponds that the victims suffered some kind of toxic poisoning administered through the mouth. Indeed, reports indicated that the family was suspected of dying from a toxin that was added to a cake.

The method of numerical interpretation used in this chapter appears complicated, but if readers can grasp a rough idea of the essential meanings of the flying stars it is not difficult to detect the possibility of telling misfortune in advance.

The Forbidden City and Chinese Prosperity

The famous Tiananmen in Beijing is the symbol of political authority in China. Its *feng shui* is therefore worth examining for its possible effect on Chinese politics and the general well-being of this vast country. The Tiananmen is in fact part of a larger group of buildings called the Forbidden City which was originally built as a palace for the Emperors of the Ming Dynasty. According to historical records, the Forbidden City was completed in the year 1420 and it is situated with its front facing exactly south and its back due north (see Fig. 19). Based on such information, I have drawn up a flying star chart which shows the *feng shui* influences the palace will receive from all directions (see Fig. 20).

The Forbidden City is an Age of Five building with the mountain star 5 at its back and the water star 5 in front. Such a configuration was clearly designed to enhance both human fortunes and financial prosperity at the time of construction. Comparing this chart with the entire layout of the Forbidden City, we can easily see that its interior designs were made in accordance with *feng shui* rules: its main buildings are located in the position of prosperous mountain stars, while its open spaces and surrounding rivers are situated under the prosperous water star of 5 and 6 in the north-east. This is to enhance prosperity during the Age of Five and the Age of Six. The architecture of the city, therefore, seems to have been designed by the capable hands of a *feng shui* expert and its influence may also explain the rise of the great

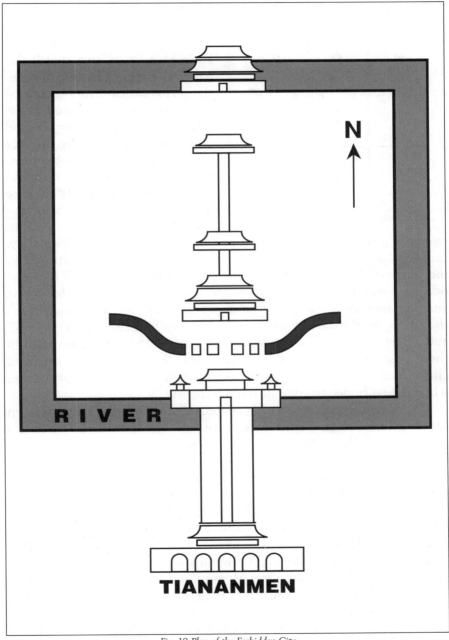

N

RIVER

TIANANMEN

Fig. 19 Plan of the Forbidden City

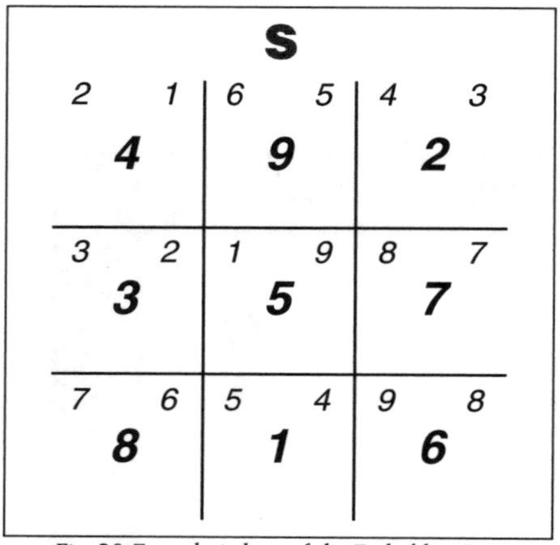

S		
2 1 6	5 4 3	
4	**9**	**2**
3 2 1	9 8 7	
3	**5**	**7**
7 6 5	4 9 8	
8	**1**	**6**

Fig. 20 Feng shui chart of the Forbidden City

Ming Dynasty, considered a golden era in Chinese history.

Nevertheless, the history of the Forbidden City shows that it also has drawbacks in its *feng shui* design. The major criticism is that the water star 9 is located in the centre of the city where we find only open space. During the Age of Five, the star 9 is not a prosperous star and placing it in water (open space) will only enhance its bad influence. Moreover, the star 9 symbolises fire and to strengthen its effect encourages fire hazards in the Forbidden City. Indeed, the records of the city show that it was repeatedly damaged by incidents of fire. Immediately after its completion in 1421, a fire occurred which burnt down its front sections, while in the following year yet another fire accident damaged the rear part. If we also check the ruling yearly stars of 1421 and 1422, we find the prevalence of 3 and 2 respectively. These two stars moved to the central position in these years to interact with the water star 9 in the original *feng shui* chart. As the star 3 symbolises wood, it naturally gives support to fire, while 2 also bodes trouble in relation to fire.

Checking through history, a clear correlation may be seen between the *feng shui* of the Forbidden City and the numerous historical upheavals in China. But it is perhaps more relevant to leave ancient history to historians and pick out some relatively recent events as examples. One obvious incident showing grave *feng shui* impact is the Cultural Revolution which occurred in the mid-1960s, during the Age of Six. At this time, many high-ranking officials in the government were dragged down from their positions to be purged and tortured by the Red Guards. To explain this period of turmoil, let us consider *feng shui* theory. Amongst the eight trigrams of the I Ching, the trigram called *Chien* (☰) symbolises Heaven and also represents the king, father or high authority. This trigram, expressed numerically, is 6 and, as we are talking about human prosperity, the emphasis is on the mountain star 6. In the *feng shui* chart of the Forbidden City we can see that the mountain star 6 is in the front entrance, forming the configuration known as "a mountain star falling into water". Moreover, the negative effect of such a configuration is most prominent when the star 6 is in a ruling position during the Age of Six. The mountain star 6 falling into water thus gives the picture of high-ranking officials falling from power and authority.

Many readers will probably be interested in seeing what *feng shui* configuration brought about the Tiananmen Square incident in 1989. The year 1989 falls into the Age of Seven and the yearly star controlling the centre is 2. However the yearly star that arrived in Tiananmen Square (which is the south entrance of the Forbidden City) was 6, again symbolic of the father or man of authority. In June, the monthly star 3, a symbol of agitation, anger and also of the son, arrived in the same position. As 6 is the metal element and 3 is wood, they are in conflict, giving a clear picture of confrontation between the government and students in June 1989.

Another interesting correlation between the flying stars of the Tiananmen and the fortune of China occurred in September 1993. In this year, the yearly star 2 and the monthly star 5 arrived in the south, in front of the Tiananmen. As mentioned previously, 2 and 5 are symbols of obstacles and misfortune. It is no wonder, then, that in this month Beijing failed in its bid to host the Olympic Games in the year 2000.

As the *feng shui* of the Forbidden City obviously has a strong impact on Chinese history, it is worth looking forward to see what lies ahead for the Chinese. As we are now in the Age of Seven, the stars we should focus on are 7 and 8, which symbolise prosperity during the next three decades. In the chart we can locate the water stars 7 and 8 in the west and north-west. Fortunately, in these two areas of the Forbidden City we also find rivers, meaning that both prosperous water stars are well placed in water. China's future prosperity can thus be guaranteed, at least until the year 2024.

The Castle Peak Explosion: A Feng Shui Investigation

On 28 August 1992, a devastating explosion occurred in a large thermal power station in Hong Kong. The accident involved the sudden explosion of the station's hydrogen production facilities and storage tanks, resulting in the death of two engineers and the injury of several workers in the vicinity. The Castle Peak Power Station had, in the past, enjoyed a reputation of efficiency and stringent safety standards. As such the accident was totally unprecedented and came as a great shock to many. The investigation into the cause of the explosion is still ongoing at the time of writing and I have made my own evaluation of its cause, based on *feng shui* theory. The result clearly shows how adverse *feng shui* influences contributed to the accident.

The Tap Shek Kok Power Station is situated in the west of Kowloon, near the Tun Mun area. The plan of the plant in Fig. 21 shows that the whole power station site, including its jetty for discharging coal vessels, is seated with its front facing the south-west and its back towards the north-east. The power station was commissioned in the early 1980s and was therefore constructed in the Age of Six. With these two pieces of information at hand, we can draw up a *feng shui* chart for the station, as illustrated in Fig. 22.

If we superimpose the chart onto a sketch of the layout of the power station, the more obvious implications are highlighted. At the back of the plant we can see the mountain star 6, while in the front, facing the Urmston Road Navigation Channel, is the water star 6.

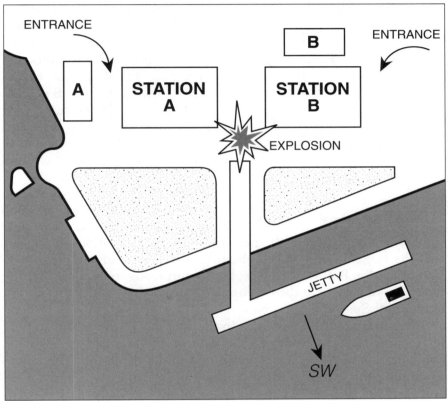

Fig. 21 Plan of the power station

Having a high mountain behind and the sea in front, the power station has a good *feng shui* configuration in both human and financial terms. However, this is only during the Age of Six, namely the years before 1984. In the Age of Seven, after 1983, the emphasis no longer falls on the stars of 6, but the stars of 7. In the chart the water star 7 is present in the north direction, while the mountain stars 7 and 8, both symbolising human prosperity, are found in the west and north-west.

The power plant is divided into two stations. The one in the north-west location is called Station A and the one in the east is called Station B. According to the *feng shui* chart regarding these locations, it is in the north-west that the benevolent mountain star 8 is situated. This symbol of human prosperity in the immediate future is also the location of the administration block for Station A. On the other hand,

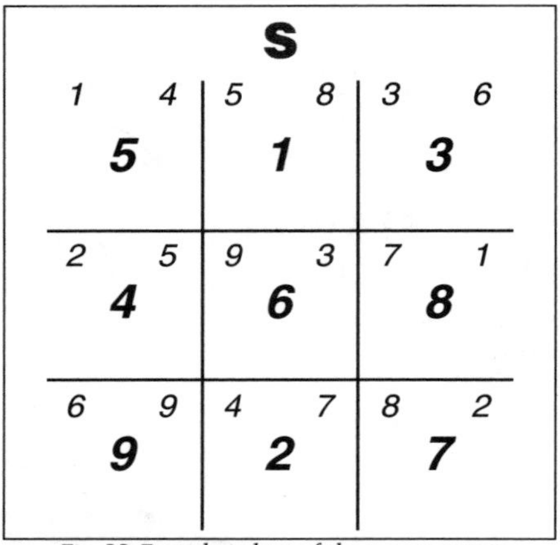

Fig. 22 Feng shui chart of the power station

the administration block for Station B is located in the east where we find the less favourable stars 2 and 5, representing troubles and obstacles. The *feng shui* advantage of site A over site B is more obvious if we also examine their respective entrances. The entrance to Station A is located in the north sector, where we find the prosperous water star 7, whereas the entrance to Station B is located in the east, presided over by the water star 5, a clear symbol of trouble. From the position of these two stations, it appears that the *feng shui* influence on Station A is comparatively superior to that of Station B. It is, therefore, hardly surprising to discover that the hydrogen tanks where the explosion occurred were under the administration of Station B.

After locating the weak spots in the *feng shui* of the power station, let us now turn our focus to the date of the accident to see what configuration of flying stars contributed to the explosion. The key to examining the actual event is to draw up a flying star chart for 28 August 1992 and see what yearly, monthly and daily stars concentrated at the key locations of the power station (see Fig. 23).

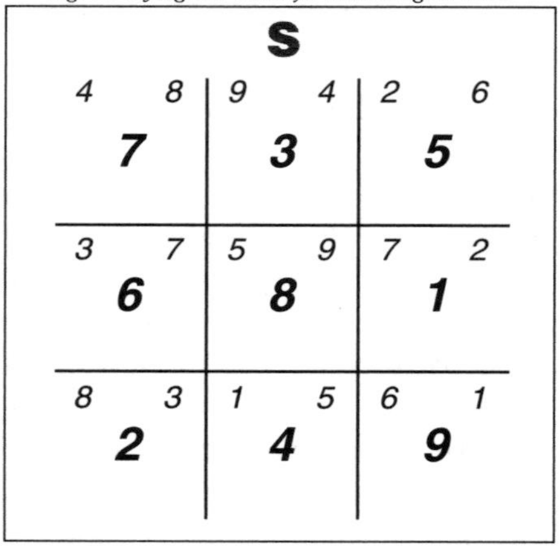

The location of the hydrogen tanks was in the centre of the power station. Therefore the flying stars that concentrated in the centre carried much weight. In the original *feng shui* chart of the station in Fig. 22, the benevolent mountain star 9 is the centre. As benevolent mountain stars need a tall building to support human prosperity, the relative emptiness and open space in the centre of

Fig. 23 Flying star chart for 28th August 1992

the station does not support the mountain star 9. The threat to human prosperity in this central location has clearly always been prominent here and it only needed the arrival of unfavourable stars like 5 and 2 to trigger an accident. The flying star chart of this particular date shows that the stars concentrating in the centre location, where the explosion occurred, are 5 and 9. As we have seen in previous chapters, 5 means trouble and mishap, while 9 is a symbol of fire. These two stars obviously interacted with the original static *feng shui* stars of 9 (fire) and 3 (conflict) to cause the explosion.

Besides looking at the location of the accident, we can also evaluate the *feng shui* configuration of the power station site as a whole in 1992. As mentioned above, the power station is seated with its back to the north-east and its front facing the south-west. In August 1992, the chart shows there was a dangerous combination of the stars 2 and 5 concentrating in the south-west, right in front of the power station. This also indicates that the power station itself was facing bad *feng shui* influences in August 1992, so a mishap eventually occurred at the point where these negative elements concentrated.

The New Hong Kong Airport

The ambitious plan of a new airport at Chek Lap Kok in the Hong Kong territories has been a controversial topic since the Governor Sir David Wilson announced the Port and Airport Development Strategy (P.A.D.S.) in 1990. The huge construction project proposes to fill up the Tung Chung Bay, rejoining Chek Lap Kok to Lantau Island, while another bridge connecting Lantau to Kowloon will provide support to the transport infrastructure. The airport itself will carry two runways, capable of handling 80 million passengers annually and with this development Lantau Island is expected to become the focus of travel and trade in Hong Kong by the year 2000.

In selecting Chek Lap Kok as the suitable site for the new airport, the consultants of the Hong Kong Government must have fully evaluated various factors, including economic and environmental feasibilities. However, the equally important *feng shui* influences affecting the prosperity of the place were probably not considered among the volumes of consultancy reports. I think it may be of interest, therefore, to provide readers with a brief outline of the *feng shui* of this important project to see how it will affect the future prosperity of Hong Kong.

As far as the physical geography of the area is concerned, focus falls on the mountains descending from Lantau peak, right in front of the airport site (see Fig. 24). The Tung Chung site is surrounded on three sides by mountain slopes, forming what *feng shui* masters call a "tiger arm" and a "dragon arm". Right in front of Tung Chung is Chek Lap

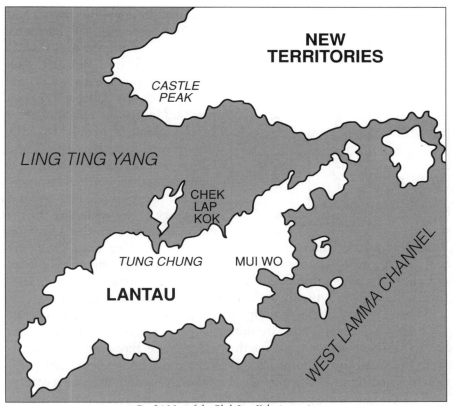

Fig. 24 Map of the Chek Lap Kok airport site

Kok Island which forms a shield to protect the land from a direct flow of water from the sea. Furthermore, the land is situated with its back to the south and its front facing the north-east towards the New Territories where we find most of Kowloon's high mountains. This kind of geographical site is referred to as a "dragon turning its head to greet the ancestors" and it is an excellent *feng shui* configuration. The Victoria Peak of Hong Kong island belongs to the same kind of configuration and is believed to have contributed tremendously towards the prosperity of the Central District in Hong Kong. The landscape of Tung Chung and Chek Lap Kok therefore qualifies as a "dragon's den", a spot where we expect to find a concentration of natural energy which generates benevolent *feng shui* influences.

However, there are two drawbacks in the original landscape which

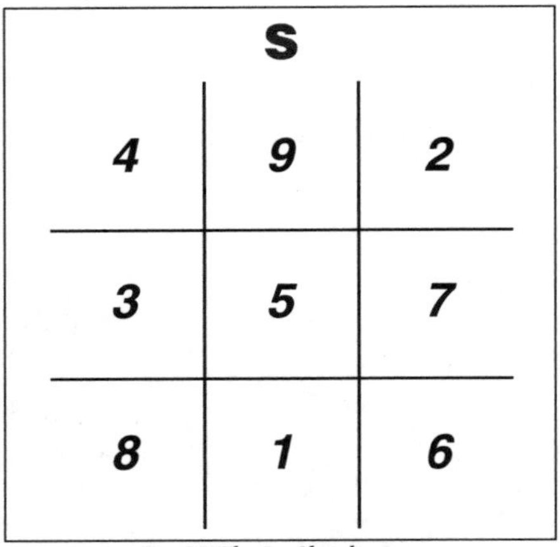

	S	
4	*9*	*2*
3	*5*	*7*
8	*1*	*6*

Fig. 25 The Lo Shu diagram

discount these various merits and which contravene the harmony that *feng shui* emphasises. Firstly, the shape of the Chek Lap Kok Island forms a spearhead pointing towards the Tung Chung. In *feng shui* terms, the weapon shape of the island is hostile towards the dragon's den in the Tung Chung site, suggesting discord and conflict, and very much hampering its prosperity. The second drawback is the widening Brothers' Channel and the Urmston Road Navigation Channel running west into the Ling Ting Yang (the sea). Such a vast expanse of flowing water with a strong current does not allow the intangible feng *shui* forces to concentrate, meaning that they will dissipate quickly and prosperity cannot be retained.

These factors, I believe, help to explain why Tung Chung has not yet been well-developed. The potential prosperity of the Lantau area has so far been superseded by the Silver Mine Bay area in the east. Here the small surrounding islands offer a more benevolent configuration by creating shields where the *feng shui* influences can concentrate.

To ascertain more precisely the future prosperity of Lantau we may apply the *Lo Shu* diagram to its landscape. This, as explained in earlier chapters, offers an evaluation of prosperity for the twenty-year duration of the Age in hand. Before doing so, however, we must remember that, if human prosperity is our focus, we will be looking for a mountain feature in the location of the number which represents the Age. On the other hand, if we wish to evaluate financial success, we must find water in the location exactly *opposite* the number representing the Age.

To illustrate this, let us first look at the landscape of Hong Kong during the Age of Six (1964 to 1983 inclusive). In the *Lo Shu* diagram (shown again in Fig. 25) this is represented by the number 6 in the north-west location. To achieve both human and economic prosperity in this twenty year period, we need to find high mountains in this north-west position and a vast expanse of water on the opposite southeast side. The landscape of Hong Kong satisfies both these conditions as it has the high Tai Mo Shan in the north-west and the sea to the south-east. Hence, Hong Kong's prosperity grew by leaps and bounds in the twenty years between 1964 and 1983, when it achieved the reputation of being a centre of world finance. However, the landscape reveals that it will not be so fortunate in the present Age of Seven (1984 to 2003 inclusive). The *Lo Shu* diagram indicates that we need high mountains in the west to sustain human prosperity and water in the east to generate wealth. If we look at the map of Hong Kong, we can see there is water in the east but no mountain in the west. This may be the *feng shui* reason behind the confidence crisis concerning the return of Hong Kong to China in 1997. In addition, a very obvious phenomenon in Hong Kong in the present Age of Seven seems to be a strong tendency for prosperous areas to move towards the east. Since 1984, the Central District seems to have gradually lost its former importance and a considerable number of commercial and residential areas are now being developed towards the east. These new areas include Admiralty, Wanchai, Kornhill and Tai Koo Shing in Hong Kong Island; and Tsim Sha Tsui Esat and Whampoa in Kowloon.

Looking ahead, after the year 2003 we will be entering the Age of Eight, which is located in the north-east of the *Lo Shu* diagram. If the above theory is correct, we can expect Hong Kong to enter a period of prosperity and economic growth, even surpassing her success in the Ages of Six and Seven. The simple reason is that in the north-east Hong Kong has huge mountain ranges, including the Ng Tung Shan, the Pat Shin Range and the Ma On Shan, all of which support her prosperity. In the opposite south-west direction there are the busy north Lantau navigation channels to generate considerable financial gains.

The most interesting and thought-provoking fact is that the new airport and the many P.A.D.S. related projects are all planned for the south-west region of Hong Kong. It seems the hands of Providence are already preparing this area to welcome the future prosperity predicted by the *Lo Shu* diagram. In line with this, we should remember that Lantau is the biggest island in Hong Kong but has been left undeveloped until the governor announced the P.A.D.S. programme in 1990. This coincides uncannily with the prediction of the 6000-year-old *Lo Shu* diagram and seems more than mere coincidence.

The Bank of China Building and the Governor's House

The most controversial and interesting *feng shui* topic in Hong Kong at present concerns the new Bank of China Building and its proximity to the Governor's House in Garden Road. The Bank of China Building is very modern and has a unique design. The upper part of this tall building is triangular in shape, with very sharp, blade-like edges. In *feng shui* theory, however, sharp or pointed objects are considered ominous and threatening. As such, the Bank of China Building may be seen as a physical *shar* on the landscape, namely a force which could cast a bad influence on surrounding constructions.

The site of the Bank of China Building is to the east of the Governor's House. If one stands at the entrance to the house, one can easily see the tall and sharp edge of the skyscraper pointing directly towards its back (see Fig. 26). Many people in Hong Kong believe this will bring bad fortune to the Governor's residence on Garden Road, a building which has always been a symbol of British rule in Hong Kong. Indeed, since the construction of the new Bank of China Building, the Governor's House has run into a series of misfortunes. Governor Sir Edward Youde died suddenly of a heart attack in 1986, while his successor, Sir David Wilson, injured himself during a morning walk. Similarly, not long after he had moved into the house, the present Governor, Chris Patten, had to cope with his daughter's hospitalisation, his wife's leg injury and his own heart operation. In addition to this, the relationship between the British and Chinese governments at

56

the time was far from harmonious.

To examine how the Bank of China Building is affecting the Governor's House, we must measure the direction of the house, find out its age and draw up a *feng shui* chart to show the influences surrounding the building. The Governor's House was first built in 1855, which makes it an Age of Nine building. However, it was substantially renovated and extended in 1890, during the Age of Two. Measuring from the Garden Road entrance of the house, we discover it faces the south-west and has its back to the north-east. Based on this information, we can draw up a *feng shui* chart as shown in Fig. 27.

The most prosperous stars in the Age of Two are the mountain star

Fig. 26 Plan of the Governor's House

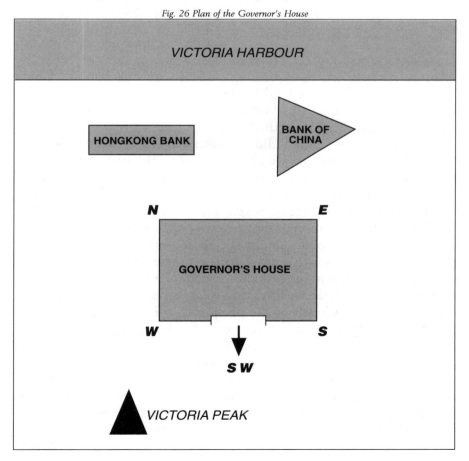

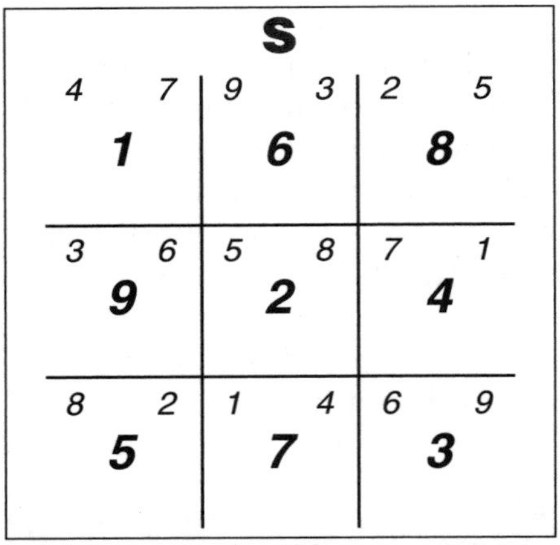

	S	
4 7 9 3 2 5		
1	**6**	**8**
3 6 5 8 7 1		
9	**2**	**4**
8 2 1 4 6 9		
5	**7**	**3**

Fig. 27 Feng shui chart of the Governor's House

2 and water star 2. We can see that the mountain star 2 is in the south-west, where the house faces the Victoria Peak, while the water star 2 is in the north-east, where Victoria Harbour's busy traffic very much enhances its power. Such a configuration means prosperity in terms of both human harmony and financial gains. This suggests the Governor's House was constructed according to *feng shui* principles which could have contributed to Hong Kong's past success. However, the theme of this chapter is the relationship between the Governor's House and the Bank of China Building, and I do not intend to discuss the overall *feng shui* of the Governor's residence. My concern is with the major problem area, namely the east location of the house.

The tall Bank of China Building is situated at the eastern corner of the Governor's House, so we should focus on the east square of the *feng shui* chart. Here we can see the pair of stars 6 and 3. The number 3 is a mountain star and 6 is a water star. The Bank of China building was completed in the Age of Seven. Prior to the construction of this building, the east location of the Governor's House offered a full view of the Victoria Harbour, unobstructed by any tall buildings. This harbour view very much enhanced the power of the water star 6, especially in the Age of Six (1964 to 1983 inclusive). As the water star 6 symbolises financial wealth, this clear harbour view in the east contributed tremendously to the prosperity of Hong Kong during the Age of Six and it was during these years that Hong Kong achieved her status as a major port and international centre of finance. After the construction of the Bank of China Building, however, the harbour view was partially shut off. Since such a tall building is regarded as a mountain, it enhances the power of the mountain star 3. According to *feng shui* symbolism, this number represents agitation and anger. The combination of 6 and 3 is, moreover, an unfavourable configuration as 6 represents metal and 3 is wood. These two elements are in conflict and they symbolise fighting, robbery and confrontation.

With the tall Bank of China Building enhancing the mountain star 3 in this way, it is not surprising to find that social and political problems have been on the increase in Hong Kong in recent years. In particular this has included a rise in the number of armed robberies and violent crime, neither of which were common in Hong Kong before 1992. This can be traced to the

S		
6	2	4
5	7	9
1	3	8

Fig. 28 Feng shui chart for 1993

influence of the mountain star 3. On the other hand, as far as financial success is concerned, Hong Kong has prospered in the Age of Seven and has not been greatly affected by the blocking of the sea view by the Bank of China Building. This is because, with the advent of the Age of Seven (after 1983) the power of the water star 6 in the Age of Six faded. It no longer represented the prosperity of the Age and thus its position on a mountain would not have such a negative influence on financial success.

In an article released to the media in early 1993, I predicted that incidents of robbery would not pose a serious threat in Hong Kong in that year, compared with 1992. This prediction has proved to be very accurate as the Hong Kong public enjoyed a more peaceful year in 1993. The secret behind my prediction was to analyse the status of the mountain star 3 in the east location of the Governor's House and see how it would be affected by the yearly star that arrived there in 1993. In this year, the star 7 moved to the centre of the square, making the star 5 move to the east location. The flying star chart for 1993 is shown in Fig. 28.

Let us focus on the east location. The yearly star 5 is an earth star, while the mountain star 3 is a wood star. Wood is the destroyer of earth. As such the wood star 3 suppresses the yearly earth star 5, in the process weakening its own power. Thus, the kinds of events symbolised by the number 3, namely robbery and conflict, could not be serious in 1993. However, as 5 is an inauspicious star and symbolises obstacles and difficulties, the combination of 3 and 5 in one location is not a good sign. I was thus able to anticipate that human conflicts of some sort would still prevail. This was exactly what happened at the beginning of 1993, when Hong Kong's crime rate improved but there was still no sign of political harmony in Sino–British relationships.

This analysis would not be complete without an examination of the possible means of dissolving the apparently negative effect of the Bank of China Building upon the *feng shui* of the Governor's House. In response to this it was rumoured that the house was inspected by a *feng shui* expert who convinced the Government to take certain *feng shui* measures that would defend it against the adverse effects of the skyscraper. This included the planting of trees and the construction of a pool, neither of which appear to have been very successful. The reason for this failure may be explained by the fact that, according to the laws governing the five elements, the shape of every object can be assigned a representative element. The nature of this element determines what kind of influence objects cast on the environment. In general, a round object represents metal, a square block is earth and a rectangular object is considered a symbol of wood. Since the tall Bank of China Building is sharp and pointed in shape, it represents the fire element. To counterbalance this fire power, it is logical that an object of earth should be used. The reason is that fire gives birth to earth and so an earth object (something in the shape of a square block) would serve to exhaust the fire energy. Any attempt to reduce the negative effect of the sharp edges of the Bank of China Building should have been based on this simple logic. The planting of trees, naturally symbolic of the wood element, only served to intensify the fire energy and encourage its negative influence.

PART 2

How to Read Destiny from Your Birth Data

In ancient Greece, Aristotle suggested that everything in the universe was made up of four elements: fire, earth, air and water. This idea was accepted in the West for two thousand years until the emergence of atomic physics examined the microscopic components of matter. Ancient Chinese metaphysics is based on a similar theory of basic elements which is perhaps much older than Greek philosophy and may even be more popular and enduring. This theory, as mentioned in the first part of this book, hinges not on four, but five elements: metal, wood, water, fire and earth. Although named after five very common tangible substances, these elements should not be interpreted in the narrow sense of their physical characteristics. Rather, they should be regarded as symbols of five fundamental forces or types of energy which are in turn governed by the Cycles of Birth and Destruction. These two laws are believed to regulate all motion and activity in the universe, based on the following interrelationship between the elements:

The Cycle of Birth: metal generates water; water gives birth to wood; wood generates fire; fire produces earth; earth completes the cycle by generating metal. This is the cycle of harmony, the cycle of the mother and child relationship.

The Cycle of Destruction: metal suppresses wood; wood conquers earth, earth stops the flow of water; water puts out fire; and fire melts metal. This cycle describes conflicting and antagonistic relationships.

The five elements are capable of a dynamic interaction which is the force behind life, activity and change in the universe. By thoroughly understanding the rules governing the relationship between the five elements, we get a deeper insight into the order, or *Tao*, of the universe. All matters, material or abstract, can be explained in this manner.

Such a philosophy is so deep-rooted in Chinese culture that its signs can be seen in all walks of life. The most obvious is the Chinese calendar which expresses years, months, days and hours in terms of the five elements. Every item – year, month, day and hour – is represented by two Chinese characters and each character symbolises one basic element. For example, the year 1993 (Year of the Rooster) can be expressed by the two Chinese characters 癸 酉 . The first character 癸 normally written on top, is called the "heavenly stem", while the second character 酉 , usually written underneath, is called an "earthly branch". There are in total ten heavenly stems and twelve earthly branches, and each of them symbolise an element. For readers who are not familiar with the Chinese calendar system, the following table lists all twenty-two characters found in it together with the corresponding element each represents.

Heavenly Stems	Earthly Branches
甲 - *Yang* wood	子 - Water (Mouse)
乙 - *Yin* wood	丑 - Earth (Ox)
丙 - *Yang* fire	寅 - Wood (Tiger)
丁 - *Yin* fire	卯 - Wood (Rabbit)
戊 - *Yang* earth	辰 - Earth (Dragon)
己 - *Yin* earth	巳 - Fire (Snake)
庚 - *Yang* metal	午 - Fire (Horse)
辛 - *Yin* metal	未 - Earth (Ram)
壬 - *Yang* water	申 - Metal (Monkey)
癸 - *Yin* water	酉 - Metal (Rooster)
	戌 - Earth (Dog)
	亥 - Water (Pig)

From this table we can gather that the year 1993, named 癸 酉 in Chinese characters, represents the influence of water and metal.

One ingenious by-product of the theory of the five elements and the Chinese calendar system is the Chinese method of fortune-telling. As the Chinese calendar can express a moment of time in terms of elements, the moment of a person's birth can also be translated into a combination of elements. This grouping or configuration of elements is believed to symbolise the composition of a person's destiny.

A person's birth data comprises four items: year, month, day and hour. As each of these items can be expressed in two Chinese characters, one above the other, a birthday expressed in Chinese is referred to as the "Four Pillars of Destiny". These pillars provide an accurate means of evaluating a person's background, character, potentials, talents, relationships with others, health and even the likely shape of the face. Those who have seriously researched this art are invariably surprised by its vast capacity to accurately describe a person and predict their future.

To explain in simple terms, this technique is based on the belief that, since the five basic elements represent the universal order and its influences, so human destiny must also be governed by the change and interaction of these elements. By knowing the rules and patterns of change, we can thus chart how the elements composing our lives react and change with the universe. This provides the key to foreseeing the pattern of our lives.

Before we can put the five basic elements into operation to predict destiny, there are two more hypotheses which readers should be familiar with. The first is the seasonal aspect of the five elements. As nature on earth changes according to the four seasons, the prosperity and strength of the basic elements also change with this natural cycle. In general, spring is the prosperous season for the wood element, as all plants prosper in springtime, while the heat of summer is associated with the fire element and is the time when fire is regarded as being most prosperous. Autumn is the season when leaves fall, so it is a time when the wood element is weak and metal, which destroys wood, becomes the strongest. Finally, in winter, water is considered the strongest element, perhaps because it is associated with ice and snow. The fifth element, earth, is regarded as neutral and so its presence is felt throughout the year. However, it is particularly strong during the last month of each season, if we divide a year equally into four seasons of three months each. The following table lists the relationship between the seasons and the five elements:

	Metal	Wood	Water	Fire
Spring	die	prosper	weak	born
Summer	born	weak	die	prosper
Autumn	prosper	die	born	weak
Winter	weak	born	prosper	die

The seasonal changes in the cycle of the five elements are fully incorporated into the Chinese calendar system. This is called the Hsia calendar as it was found to be in existence as early as the Hsia Dynasty (c. 2200 B.C.) It is a solar calendar, closely related to the movement of the earth around the sun on the imaginary circle called the "ecliptic". The year commences on the first day of spring, which normally falls on 4 or 5 February in the Western calendar and ends on the last day of winter when the earth completes its cycle. So the twelve months of the year are formed by dividing the ecliptic into twelve portions which are named according to the twelve earthly branches. For instance, the first day of the first month of the year (around 4 February) is expressed by the earthly branch symbolising the wood element. The relationship between the Hsia and Western calendars is listed below.

Hsia Months		Element	Season	Western Months
1	寅	Wood	Spring	4, 5 Feb – 5, 6 Mar
2	卯	Wood	Spring	5, 6 Mar – 4, 5 Apr
3	辰	Earth	Spring	4, 5 Apr – 5, 6 May
4	巳	Fire	Summer	5, 6 May – 5, 6 June
5	午	Fire	Summer	5, 6 June – 7, 8 July
6	未	Earth	Summer	7, 8 July – 7, 8 Aug
7	申	Metal	Autumn	7, 8 Aug – 7, 8 Sept
8	酉	Metal	Autumn	7, 8 Sept – 8, 9 Oct
9	戌	Earth	Autumn	8, 9 Oct – 7, 8 Nov
10	亥	Water	Winter	7, 8 Nov – 7, 8 Dec
11	子	Water	Winter	7, 8 Dec – 5, 6 Jan
12	丑	Earth	Winter	5, 6 Jan – 4, 5 Feb

The table shows that the Chinese calendar also incorporates the influence of one of the five basic elements in each month. For example, spring is considered to be a month when plants prosper, so the first two months of the spring season are symbolised by earthly branches representing the wood element. Similarly, summer is a hot season in the northern hemisphere, so it is represented by the earthly branches of fire. Readers may also note that the third month of each season is symbolised by an earth element since earth is considered a neutral element, the inflence of which will prevail throughout the year.

Besides the year, month and day, the Hsia calendar also expresses the 24 hours of the day in terms of the elements represented by the heavenly stems and earthly branches. However, as there are only twelve earthly branches, the Chinese have to group two hours together to make one, thus forming a system of only twelve hours. The following table shows the twelve-hour system of the Hsia calendar.

Hsia Hours		Animal	Element	Western Time
1	子	Rat	Water	2300 – 0100
2	丑	Ox	Earth	0100 – 0300
3	寅	Tiger	Wood	0300 – 0500
4	卯	Rabbit	Wood	0500 – 0700
5	辰	Dragon	Earth	0700 – 0900
6	巳	Snake	Fire	0900 – 1100
7	午	Horse	Fire	1100 – 1300
8	未	Goat	Earth	1300 – 1500
9	申	Monkey	Metal	1500 – 1700
10	酉	Rooster	Metal	1700 – 1900
11	戌	Dog	Earth	1900 – 2100
12	亥	Pig	Water	2100 – 2300

Hence the Hsia calendar enables us to express any moment of time, including year, month, day and hour, in terms of the elements of the heavenly stems and earthly branches. By doing so we are able to see what elemental influence the universe will cast on human fortune at any moment of time, either in the past or the future. We can thus make predictions about the future by evaluating the impact of such elemental forces on our birth data. To offer an example of this, the following is a sample set of four pillars obtained by converting the birth data of the rock star Elvis Presley into the Hsia calendar.

Hour Pillar	Day Pillar	Month Pillar	Year Pillar	
丙	甲	丁	甲	*Heavenly Stems*
Fire	Wood	Fire	Wood	
寅	申	丑	戌	*Earthly Branches*
Wood	Metal	Earth	Earth	

Luck Pillars

39	29	19	9	*Age*
辛	庚	己	戊	*Heavenly Stems*
Metal	Metal	Earth	Earth	
巳	辰	卯	寅	*Earthly Branches*
Fire	Earth	Wood	Wood	

The Pillars of Destiny of Elvis Presley

Elvis Presley was born on 8 January 1935 at 3.30 a.m. We can see that every item in his birth data, when converted to the Hsia calendar, can be expressed in Chinese characters which symbolise basic elements. The characters on top are heavenly stems and those below are earthly branches. This set of eight characters therefore represents the elemental composition of a person's destiny. However, besides the hour, day, month and year pillars, we may draw information about a persons's change in fortune from what we call his "luck pillars". Luck pillars are double Chinese characters derived from the month pillar and each one represents the elemental influences in a person's destiny for a ten-year period. The small numbers at the top of each luck pillar indicate the age at which a person will come under that pillar's influence.

Even with this theoretical background, we still need a method which will convert the five simple elements into matters relating to our complicated daily lives. To do this we firstly find the element present on the heavenly stem of the day of birth. This is referred to as the "self" and from this starting point we may apply the Cycles of Birth and Destruction to the five elements. Through this is revealed the complicated interrelationship between the self and life. For instance, a person born on a day when the heavenly stem is represented by wood is by definition a "wood person". If we wish to focus on this person through his personal relationships, we find that his mother, for example, would be symbolised by water as this is the element which gives birth to wood. Similarly, assuming the wood person is male, his wife would be represented by the element conquered by wood, namely earth. This is because women were traditionally considered the weaker sex, to be conquered by the male. Consequently, any element which a self-sign conquers symbolises the wife of a male subject.

We can also apply this theory to matters beyond human relationships. For instance, the knowledge and resourcefulness of a wood person is represented by water, as this element, in a maternal fashion, nourishes and supports the growth of wood. Similarly, as the Cycle of Destruction describes wood conquering earth, earth becomes a wood person's achievements or rewards, in short his symbol of wealth.

Such relationships between the elements and human life may seem complicated, but they are in fact logical deductions which seem to adhere closely to normal human customs and relationships. For clarity, the following table lists these interrelationships, using a wood male as an example.

Elements	People	Significance
wood	self	colleagues, competition
water	mother	resources, support, authority
earth	wife, father	wealth, money
metal	son	status, pressure, power
fire	–	intelligence, expression

At first glance it may not be easy to understand why earth symbolises the father of a wood person or why metal is his son. The process is one of logical deduction. Water represents the mother as it gives birth to wood. The element which conquers water is earth. Therefore earth is the husband of the mother and hence the father of the wood person. Similarly, a wood person's wife is represented by the earth element as this is conquered by wood. The earth element gives birth to metal, so metal thereby becomes the symbol of the son.

A table of relationships for each of the five elements can be found in *Appendix 2* of this book, but it would be a test of understanding if readers could attempt to deduce the relationships for their own elemental sign before turning to this.

Having equipped readers with these fundamental theories, I may now go on to demonstrate the very real significance of the Four Pillars of Destiny. In order to gain a deeper insight into the actual operation of destiny analysis, the rest of this book uses a wide selection of famous and prominent people as examples and shows in practical terms how birth data, expressed in elements, can accurately assess and predict the pattern of life.

Li Ka-shing – Destiny of a Billionaire

Mr Li Ka-shing, the property tycoon and chairman of the giant Cheung Kwong Corporation and Hutchison Group, tops the list of Hong Kong billionaires in terms of the wealth under his control. It is well known that Mr Li is a self-made man, born of a poor family in mainland China. Nevertheless, his spectacular business success over the past years has astonished many and earned him the nickname "The Superman of Business". Mr Li Ka-shing is known to be an intelligent and hard-working person, qualities which must certainly have contributed to his rise to the top. However, not all dedicated and intelligent people have achieved Mr Li's kind of success and we cannot deny that luck must also have been a very important, if not indispensable factor in his life story. While many consider luck to be an uncertain and irrational element in life, beyond our control, the ancient art of the Four Pillars of Destiny casts a logical light on this phenomenon.

This chapter will specifically demonstrate how Mr Li Ka-shing's good fortune can be explained through his birth data, expressed in the Pillars of Destiny. The analysis will also cover a wider scope of information, including how the Four Pillars can reveal the appropriate direction of career development; the field of business one is likely to enter; the positive and negative aspects of human relationships; as well as the general fluctuations in personal fortune.

Firstly, let us consider Mr Li's Pillars of Destiny. Mr Li was born on 13 June 1928. While the actual hour of his birth is unknown, the following shows the remaining three pillars of this date.

	Hour	Day	Month	Year
		甲	戊	戊
	?	Wood	Earth	Earth
		申	午	辰
	?	Metal	Fire	Earth

68	58	48	38	28	18	8
乙	甲	癸	壬	辛	庚	己
Wood	Wood	Water	Water	Metal	Metal	Earth
丑	子	亥	戌	酉	申	未
Earth	Water	Water	Earth	Metal	Metal	Earth

The Pillars of Destiny of Li Ka-shing

When examining these pillars, the first rule to remember is that the element on the heavenly stem of the day when a person was born symbolises the person himself, while the other elements in the year, month and hour represent his relationships with other people or his surroundings. By definition, then, we can consider Mr Li a man of the wood element, born in the summer season in a month of fire.

Mr Li is a symbol of wealth in Hong Kong and it is natural that money should occupy a prominent position in his destiny. As wealth is something that one conquers and acquires, it is represented by the element that one's self-sign destroys. In Mr Li's case, wood destroys earth, so earth becomes the symbol of his wealth. Readers can immediately see the prominence of earth elements in Mr Li's pillars. As he was born in the summer when the fire element is the strongest, the strength and significance of earth is further intensified as fire gives birth to earth.

One interesting aspect of the Pillars of Destiny is that they can provide instruction on the most fruitful field in which to invest one's talents. In Mr Li's case, since wood feeds and generates fire, fire symbolises his intelligence and aspirations. The strong presence of fire and earth in the configuration shows that Mr Li possesses great talent in generating wealth out of earth. Consequently, the most fruitful field for him to work in is one which involves land, namely the property business.

A more astonishing aspect of the Four Pillars is that they can vividly display the pattern of fortune throughout a person's life. This is achieved by adding to the birth data a list of elements called "luck pillars" which are derived from the month of birth. Each luck pillar contains two elements and governs a person's fortune for ten years. The small number at the top of each luck pillar shows the age a person will be when under the influence of that particular pillar.

To chart the history of Mr Li's success through his luck pillars, it is necessary to determine which element will bring him good fortune and which will bring misfortune and setbacks. Mr Li's day pillar shows he is a wood person born in a month of fire. As wood generates fire and fire exhausts wood energy, we can consider Mr Li a weak wood person. The philosophy behind the Four Pillars of Destiny, however, is harmony and balance, so it is generally undesirable if any element in a set of four pillars is either too weak or excessively strong. In the case of a very weak element, it is necessary to improve its strength with other supportive elements. On the other hand, if an element is too strong, its excessive energy should be controlled or exhausted. As Mr Li's wood element is weak, he needs the support of water which will provide the wood with necessary nourishment. Metal generates water, so it is also a favourable element. Hence we can postulate that his good fortunes will be supported by metal and water. On the other hand, fire and earth are antagonistic elements which will not be supportive of success. Bearing this postulation in mind, let us examine Mr Li's luck pillars to see if they match well with the mammoth successes of his past.

Just as the day pillar symbolises the person himself, the month pillar symbolises a person's parents and family background. In Mr Li's case, the month pillar is occupied by earth and fire elements which we know are not supportive of the wood. Indeed, Mr Li was born into a poor mainland Chinese family. His father died early in his childhood and his mother could only support him long enough to complete two years of formal education. The unfavourable earth element continued to prevail in Mr Li's first luck pillar between the age of eight and seventeen, so he was still in the clutches of poverty when he came to Hong Kong at the age of eleven. However, his fortune turned considerably after he entered the luck pillar of metal at the age of eighteen. At this age he started work as a salesman in a small machine factory and was rapidly promoted to manager in 1948, a year of water. The luck pillar of metal continued to generate support by providing water nourishment to his wood and in 1950, a year of wood, Mr Li became the owner of a small factory manufacturing plastic flowers.

The favourable changes caused by the influence of metal in his youth are also reflected by the metal element found in the earthly branch of his day pillar. This position is often referred to as the "house of the spouse" as it symbolises a man's relationship with his wife. The presence of metal, a favourable element, in this position also reveals that Mr Li received firm support from his wife. Indeed, it is said that Mrs Li was a well-educated and capable lady who provided her husband with valuable encouragement during his early years in business.

At the age of 38, Mr Li entered another favourable luck pillar presided over by the water element. During this period he made some very wise decisions to invest in property at a time when the Hong Kong market was at a low due to the banking troubles of 1964 and the civil disturbance of 1967. Consequently, by the time he moved into his next luck pillar of pure water at the age of 48, Mr Li was already a property tycoon with the gigantic Cheung Kwong Development Company, listed in the Stock Exchange in 1972 – a year of the favourable water element. Since water is Mr Li's auspicious element, the luck pillar of water between the ages of 48 and 58 could be considered his golden era of greatest success. With the assistance of some favourable years in the 1970s, he astonished the property world by annexing large corporations like Hutchison International into his Cheung Kwong Empire.

It is hardly necessary to go through Mr Li's great achievements since the age of 48. The fact I wish to stress to readers is that his success is so consistent with what is reflected in his Pillars of Destiny. He is a man born with the potential to possess great wealth (earth) and he has made good use of his innate potentials and talents (fire). Furthermore, the consecutive luck pillars of strong metal and water provided him with the resources and strength to manipulate the earth and fire. All these factors constitute the destiny of a great business-man.

More recently, the years 1992 and 1993 were also years of strong metal and water influence, both of which are supportive of his success. It appears, therefore, that Mr Li will remain very much in the fore-ground of the Hong Kong business world before he leaves the present luck pillar of water at the age of 68.

Sir Yue Kong Pao and the Water Element

Another Hong Kong billionaire, second only to Mr Li Ka-shing in his wealth and success, was the shipping and property magnate, the late Sir Yue Kong Pao, commonly known as "Mr Supertanker". The following Pillars of Destiny belong to Sir Yue Kong.

	Hour	Day	Month	Year
	?	辛 Metal	癸 Water	戊 Earth
	?	酉 Metal	亥 Water	午 Fire

79	69	59	49	39	29	19	9
辛 Metal	庚 Metal	己 Earth	戊 Earth	丁 Fire	丙 Fire	乙 Wood	甲 Wood
未 Earth	午 Fire	巳 Fire	辰 Earth	卯 Wood	寅 Wood	丑 Earth	子 Water

The Pillars of Destiny of Sir Yue Kong Pao

The uniqueness of Sir Yue Kong's pillars lies in their orderly configuration, which shows the earthly branches firmly supporting each heavenly stem. The pillars are metal on metal, water on water and earth on fire, with the element underneath clearly supporting the element above. This reflects a stable person who has determination and strong will-power. It may also explain why Sir Yue Kong was known for his conservatism and was respected as a genuine industrialist and investor in the business world. Moreover, the abundant water flow, supported by strong metal, also symbolises great creativity and resourcefulness.

Sir Yue Kong's day pillar portrays him as a strong metal man born in the winter season when water is most prosperous. As metal and water are elements of the autumn and winter seasons, their presence creates a "cold" configuration, especially in-

tensified by the fact that Sir Yue Kong was born in winter in northern China. We have already discussed the importance of maintaining harmony and balance among the elements of the Four Pillars in order to avoid excessive strengths or weaknesses. But, besides this balancing of power, it is equally necessary to achieve a balance of temperature in the configuration, as intense heat or cold are again indicative of disharmony. For instance, if a set of pillars is considered "cold" due to the strong presence of metal and water, it is favourable to have the fire element providing more warmth and reducing the coldness. Following this, Sir Yue Kong's most favourable elements would therefore be fire and earth. Fire not only provides warmth, but also generates earth which in turn supports the metal day pillar. The Chinese further believe that, as metal needs fire to turn it into useful tools, fire may be regarded as catalyst to a metal person's success and can thus indicate the most auspicious direction for personal development. As the south is considered to be the direction where fire is most prosperous, it is not surprising to find that Sir Yue Kong achieved great success after he headed south from Shanghai and came to Hong Kong to develop his business.

Having established that fire and earth are Sir Yue Kong's auspicious elements, it is logical to deduce that water, threatening to extinguish fire, is an unfavourable element. Moreover, metal, helping to generate excessive water, is even worse. With these relationships in mind, it will be interesting to see if Sir Yue Kong's path to success was consistent with the working of these elements.

Let us take a closer look at the configuration of Sir Yue Kong's pillars. He was born in winter and, since there are two water elements in his month pillar, naturally the most prominent element in the three known pillars is water. Water is the off-spring of metal, so for a metal person water symbolises creativity and intelligence. On the other hand, metal conquers wood, so wood is a symbol of wealth to a man of metal. In the three known pillars of Sir Yue Kong, however, the element of wood is lacking. Nevertheless, as water is the mother of wood, the presence of strong water in Sir Yue Kong's destiny reflects his great potential to generate wood (money). This water influence also explains why he was able to acquire such immense wealth from his fleet of supertankers, for which he was nicknamed "The King of the Sea." Clearly, water is his money-generating element.

Sir Yue Kong's year pillar, in contrast, is occupied by the favourable earth and fire elements. Earth is the mother of metal, and symbolizes his resourcefulness, while fire conquers metal and represents status and power. Therefore the prominence of the earth and fire elements in the year pillar fully reflects that Sir Yue Kong was not only a great business man, but also a man of good reputation and high status. Indeed, he maintained close friendships with many heads of states and politicians, as well as taking chairmanship of several maritime organizations.

Just as the day pillar represents the self and the month pillar symbolises the parents, by the same token the year pillar reflects the influence of the grandparents' generation or beyond. The favourable fire element in his year pillar shows that Sir Yue Kong possessed a very good family background which can be traced back at least to his grandfather's generation. However, Sir Yue Kong does not owe his success to his father, as the month pillar, representing the parent, is occupied by the unfavourable water element. Indeed, it is said that the young Sir Yue Kong started his career as a bank manager and that his father initially objected to his switching to the shipping business. In fact, he bought his first vessel, the *M. V. Golden Alfa*, with his own savings in 1955, a year of earth when he was in a favourable luck pillar of fire. Nevertheless, one must not discount the great respect that Sir Yue Kong had for his father. This relationship is clearly reflected in the fact that the water elements appearing in the month pillar (representing the father) are closely supported by metal, Sir Yue Kong's own sign.

From his past luck pillars one can see that Sir Yue Kong was constantly under the good influence of fire and earth from the age of 39 to 69, during which time his fleet of bulk carriers and supertankers grew rapidly. However, I do not think it is necessary to go into further detail about his great successes in the shipping field in the 1970s and the property business in the 1980s. Rather more interesting is an explanation of a particularly unique feature of Sir Yue Kong's pillars. This feature addresses two issues: firstly, why he should have chosen shipping as a career, despite the unfavourable presence of water in his destiny; and, secondly, why he changed his focus from shipping to property in the 1980's.

In the previous chapter we saw that Mr Li Ka-shing was surrounded by the earth element in his pillars which made him destined to derive his fortune from the property (earth) business. Similarly, Sir Yue Kong's pillars show metal and water elements to be the most prominent, thus suggesting that he was driven by the strong water influence in his destiny to enter the shipping (water and metal) business. However, when he reached the age of 59, he entered a luck pillar of strong fire and earth influence. Naturally the earth influence prevailed over water and it was then that he switched his investments to property. This hypothesis clearly shows that the direction of our career paths is determined more by the element of strongest influence than simply the favourable element in our destinies.

Sir Yue Kong unfortunately died in 1991 at the age of 73. At this time he was in a luck pillar presided over by metal. His actual date of death was also a day of metal in a month of metal. In addition to this, Sir Yue Kong died of a sickness related to the breathing organs, a part of the body associated with the metal element. These facts provide unanimous evidence that, despite a lifetime of unquestionable career success in the shipping (metal) industry, metal was an unfavourable element for this great shipping magnate.

Ronald Li
and the
Hong Kong
Stock Market

Having analysed the destinies of two billionaires, a
property tycoon and a
shipping magnate, I now
propose to consider the
fortune of yet another
type of entrepreneur.
Mr Ronald Li, the
former chairman of the
Hong Kong Stock Ex-
change, acquired his
great wealth through
the more volatile busi-
ness of stocks and shares.

In the previous two
analyses, it was quite obvious that the earth element
could represent the property
industry, while water and
metal could symbolise shipping. But, unlike property
and shipping, finance is a
more abstract business and

cannot immediately be identified with a particular element. It is therefore worth examining the Pillars of Destiny of people who have excelled on the stock exchange, since the element contributing to their success may provide us with hints about the elemental nature of this field of business. The following Pillars of Destiny belong to Mr Ronald Li.

	Hour	Day	Month	Year
		丙	丙	己
	?	Fire	Fire	Earth
		戌	寅	巳
	?	Earth	Wood	Fire

72	62	52	42	32	22	12	2
戊	己	庚	辛	壬	癸	甲	乙
Earth	Earth	Metal	Metal	Water	Water	Wood	Wood
午	未	申	酉	戌	亥	子	丑
Fire	Earth	Metal	Metal	Earth	Water	Water	Earth

The Pillars of Destiny of Ronald Li

Mr Li is a fire person born in early spring when the element of wood is most prosperous. This strong wood influence provides nourishment to the fire, which is prominent in all three known pillars. Mr Li is therefore a very strong fire person. As his destiny possesses such a strong fire influence and his major business success is in the stock market and finance, it is not difficult for us to deduce that fire is the element associated with the stock exchange. Moreover, Mr Li's acquisition or "conquering" of wealth is represented by the relationship of fire destroying or conquering metal, this latter element thereby becoming his symbol of wealth.

While the three known pillars of Mr Li do not possess any prominent metal element, we can see that a great potential to produce wealth is present. Firstly, metal is generated by earth, so the earth element represents both his innate financial wisdom and the initial capitol investment required to generate wealth. There are indeed two prominent earth elements in Mr Li's pillars, showing that the money-making mechanism is certainly there. Secondly, to become a billion-aire, one must also possess the strength to manipulate wealth. If the self-sign is weak, too much wealth or too many wealth-generating elements, will only further weaken the self, upsetting the elemental balance and bringing about trouble. Mr Li's pillars show he is a very strong fire person and that he possesses the capacity to gain and control wealth once he encounters it in his passage through life. All he needs is an auspicious luck pillar to bring him under the influence of metal, his symbol of wealth.

Such an opportunity came at the age of 42, when Mr Li stepped into a ten-year luck pillar of pure metal. By comparison, the first four luck pillars of water and earth, which prevailed before the age of 42, were rather ordinary. Following his graduation from the University of Pennsylvania, he had attempted to become a public accountant. How-ever, in 1969, a year of metal, his luck changed and he began to set up the Far East Stock Exchange. It was in the following years, especially after entering two luck pillars of metal at the age of 42 and 52, that he really displayed his genius as a financial wizard on the stock market. He managed not only to orchestrate the merging of Hong Kong's four stock exchanges, but to make the Far East Stock Exchange one of Asia's most dynamic markets, raising Hong Kong to the position of a major international financial centre. This beneficial metal influence culminated in his chairmanship of the unified Hong Kong Stock Exchange in 1986 at the age of 57.

Readers can clearly see that the golden era of Mr Li's career, between the age of 47 and 52, was presided over by metal (both in his luck pillars and the years of his success), while his achievements on the stock market are closely associated with the strong fire element. Un-fortunately, however, Mr Li was sentenced to jail for commercial fraud in October of 1990 which was a Year of the Horse, a year of metal on fire. The fire element is known to be prosperous in the summer season, but its effect gradually declines towards autumn and winter. Its life-cycle is indeed considered to reach a stage of "imprison-ment" in October and it totally dies away in November and Decem-ber. This rapid fading of the fire influence in October of 1990 had a grave impact on many people whose Pillars of Destiny had been relying on the fire element in the years preceding 1990. The most dramatic example was the resignation of Mrs Thatcher, the metal lady whose fire element (a symbol of her power and authority) was extinguished in November. Yet Mrs Thatcher was not the only casualty of the dying fire element. The fluctuations in the influence of the elements can effect the destinies of whole organizations as well as individuals. We may apply this to the stock market itself to see how its fortunes and those of Mr Li are so closely entwined.

Earlier, I mentioned that the fire element is a symbol of the stock market. This postulation is not only derived from the destiny of Mr Li, but is also made on the basis of the record of Wall Street performances. In the past, the prosperity of the fire element often brought about a "bullish" market. The fire influence peaked in 1986, a year of strong wood and fire, which brought a boom to most industries and stocks. This continued in 1987, again a year of fire. However, in October 1987, the global stock market took a nosedive due to the transition from this dominating fire influence to a year of strong earth (1988). The loss of fire effect in the autumn of 1987 caused the stock market to collapse in October and also brought about a dramatic change in fortune for Mr Li, who relied very much on the fire element for his business successes. Previously, his fire element had gained support and nourishment from the wood presiding in his month pillar which in turn gave his fire enough strength to manipulate metal, his wealth. In this way, we may consider his ability to control finances as reliant not only on the strength of fire, but on the balancing support of wood. The presence of wood in his month pillar is therefore of paramount importance in acting as a life-supporter and the hinge of balance and harmony in his destiny. Once removed, his configuration of elements becomes upset, causing turmoil and trouble.

This is precisely what occurred in 1987 when Mr Li was 58. In this year he entered the earthly branch of his luck pillar presided over by *yang* metal, which clashed with the wood element in the earthly branch of his month pillar. Such a conflict resulted in the destruction of his life-supporting wood, making his fire influence so weak that he could no longer manipulate his metal wealth. Losing the support of wood, he had to survive by relying totally on the external fire element presiding over the years 1987 and 1990. The demise of the fire element put Mr Li in a weak position and compelled his decision to close the Hong Kong stock market for four days. The subsequent drop of over one thousand points in the Hang Seng Index caused great controversy and Mr Li was arrested on bribery charges in early 1988, a year of earth which further exhausted his fire strength. However, the years 1989 (earth and fire) and the early part of 1990 (metal and fire) were periods when fire regained strength and it seemed things improved for Mr Li. There was even optimism that the charges against him might be dropped. However, the cyclical change of fire into metal and water in October 1990 once again let him down. Interestingly, it was rumoured that a *feng shui* expert advised Mr Li to wear a red tie during his appearances in court. However, such a symbol of fire was too weak to rescue him from his resulting imprisonment, brought about by the passing of the fire influence at the close of the Year of the Horse.

The U. S. Presidential Election: Bush vs Clinton

The international event that captured most public attention in 1992 was the U.S. Presidential Election held in November. As the big date drew near, the various popularity polls conducted by the U.S. media showed results overwhelmingly in favour of the Democrat, Bill Clinton. It is interesting to make an evaluation of the pillars of both candidates to see whether the results of the election were already pre-ordained in destiny.

Mr Bush was born on 12 June 1924. His pillars are as follows.

	Hour	Day	Month	Year	
	?	壬 Water	庚 Metal	甲 Wood	
	?	戌 Earth	午 Fire	子 Water	
68	58	48	38	28	18
丁 Fire	丙 Fire	乙 Wood	甲 Wood	癸 Water	壬 Water
丑 Earth	子 Water	亥 Water	戌 Earth	酉 Metal	申 Metal

The Pillars of Destiny of George Bush

Mr Bush's birthday was a day of water in the summer season, when the fire element is most prosperous. He is therefore regarded as a water man, even though water is not "in season" in a summer month and is here sitting on its destroyer, earth. As such, it is very weak in strength. Fortunately, in this case, the water has taken root in another water element in his year pillar, while close support is provided by the metal in his month pillar. As metal generates water, these elements are supportive and provide resources for Mr Bush's water energy. However, weighing the strength of all the elements in the configuration, he is still a weak water person as the elements of fire and earth, which exhaust water power, are very prominent. In summary, he requires the supportive strength of the favourable water and metal elements, while fire and earth, their respective destroyers, are antagonistic and bound to bring problems and obstacles.

Applying this to Mr Bush's past, we discover the hypothesis to be quite accurate. His month pillar, symbolising his upbringing and relationship with his father, reflects both a good family background and paternal support since it is occupied by the favourable metal element which generates water. Indeed, Mr Bush's father, Prescott Shelton Bush, was a prominent banker on Wall Street and a respected senator. Other personal relation-

87

ships also support our theory. When Mr Bush married Barbara Pierce in 1944, he was only 20 years old and under the influence of water on metal in his luck pillar. In addition, 1944 was a year of metal and these two facts indicate a happy and lasting marriage.

The events which occurred during President Bush's leadership again match very well with our hypothesis that metal brings him good fortune, while fire and earth represent obstacles. For instance, in 1990 the year sign of fire clashed with the water in the President's year pillar. His birth configuration is therefore said to "offend the Grand Duke of the year" and such a situation usually means challenges, pressure and obstacles. Indeed, it was in this Year of the Horse that President Bush had to face an international crisis situation brought about by the Iraqi invasion of Kuwait in August. In contrast, 1991, a favourable year of metal, saw the President achieving great success in foreign affairs by winning the Gulf War and liberating Kuwait. In the same year he also ended the Cold War against the U.S.S.R., which saw a total reshuffle in the balance of power in favour of the U.S. Under the supporting influence of metal, President Bush glorified his country and regained a national pride which had been lost in America since the Korean and the Vietnamese wars.

Moving to 1992, the Year of the Monkey was one of strong water and metal, President Bush's favouring elements. This gave him a good chance of winning the forthcoming election. However, the impact of a year only gives the short-term benefits. We must also examine the luck pillars which affect a person in the long-term and which indicate the direction of his future development. At the age of 68, President Bush left the favourable luck pillar of water and moved into the less beneficial pillar of fire. This considerably discounted the positive effects he received from the water and metal in this year. Moreover, assessing the result of the election is not simply a case of examining Mr Bush's personal destiny. The outcome of such a struggle for power and authority is necessarily effected both by the destiny of his competitor and the kind of external influences the date of the actual event brought.

This latter factor involves examining the implications of the Year of the Monkey on Mr Bush's position and power. Being a water person, power is symbolised by the earth element which destroys water. The year 1992 is one of strong metal and water which do not offer any support to earth. Additionally, as the President is a weak water person and the Year of the Monkey is a strong water year, the emphasis on this element in the year may represent the emergence of a competitor who is considerably stronger than him in the struggle for power. In summary, while the elemental nature of 1992 was generally positive for Mr Bush, its influence also carried with it the suggestion that, in the field of competition and status, his strength would be second best.

Of course, the other factor we cannot ignore in examining the election is the destiny of Mr Bill Clinton. Mr Bill Clinton's birth data is expressed in Pillars of Destiny as follows.

Hour	Day	Month	Year
	乙	丙	丙
?	Wood	Fire	Fire
	丑	申	戌
?	Earth	Metal	Earth

The Pillars of Destiny of Bill Clinton

As the pillars show, Mr Clinton is a very weak wood person, born in autumn in a month when metal is most prosperous. As metal destroys wood, Mr Clinton's wood is so weak that he has to totally give up his wood property and surrender to metal. Therefore metal, meaning power and position to him, will be his favourable element. As such, the Year of the Monkey (a year of metal) was certainly very positive for Mr Clinton and gave him a good chance of gaining power and authority. Comparing his pillars to those of Mr Bush, the balance appears to swing in favour of Mr Clinton in 1992, especially as the date of the election (3 November 1992) happened to fall in a month of strong metal. Mr Clinton's Pillars of Destiny in fact belong to a special type of configuration called "Follow the Leader", explained in detail in the chapter dealing with the destiny of Mr K. P. Yung. In conclusion, then, there was nothing wrong with President Bush's fortunes in 1992, except that his competitor was too strong and the election fell on an unfavourable day.

A Profile of Governor Chris Patten

In April 1992 the much-awaited appointment of the new Governor for Hong Kong was announced in London. The choice of Mr Chris Patten caused mixed feelings among Hong Kong's people. Mr Patten was the former Chairman of the Conservative Party and the Hong Kong media generally welcomed him as a heavyweight politician with close ties to the Prime Minister. Some thought that such a background might add to his authority in handling

SARA -'92

Hong Kong affairs. However, others considered him naive of the Hong Kong situation and inexperienced in foreign diplomacy. How he would perform in his new job could only remain to be seen.

In the first six months of his appointment it seemed that Mr Patten was indeed a capable diplomat, presenting himself well to the Hong Kong people. However, in the last quarter of 1992, his bold political reform proposals stimulated a row between the British and Chinese governments over Hong Kong's future after 1997. The international controversy which followed placed Mr Patten in a very difficult situation and came as a major setback to his credibility and achievements as Governor. With this in mind, it is interesting to examine his birth data to find out more about the man and how destiny has effected his political career. Whether the British administration in Hong Kong can continue to function effectively depends very much on the leadership of the Governor. His personal luck in the coming years will therefore play an important role and in this respect the Pillars of Destiny may provide some answers.

Mr Patten was born on 12 May 1944. He is therefore a man of fire, born in the summer season. As fire is most prosperous in summer, he is considered a strong fire person. This fire power is further strengthened by the prominent wood element on the heavenly stem of his year pillar.

	Hour	Day	Month	Year
		丙	己	甲
	?	Fire	Earth	Wood
		子	巳	申
	?	Water	Fire	Metal

58	48	38	28	18	8
乙	甲	癸	壬	辛	庚
Wood	Wood	Water	Water	Metal	Metal
亥	戌	酉	申	未	午
Water	Earth	Metal	Metal	Earth	Fire

The Pillars of Destiny of Governor Chris Patten

Yang fire symbolises the brilliant sun and energy. Therefore a person of strong fire often has a positive and energetic personality. He is likely to be active, open-minded and outspoken, possessing the warmth and the charisma of the sun. Moreover, a strong fire person generally has guts, ambition and is certainly not what local people refer to as a *kowtow* man (a yes-man). Like all men of forceful character, a strong fire person is also known to be stubborn and occasionally hot-tempered.

As we are now familiar with, the heavenly stem of the Pillars of Destiny represents the personality and outlook of a person. In the case of Mr Patten, they are shown as the fire, earth and wood elements. Wood is the mother and fuel of fire, so the *yang* wood on the year pillar represents the wisdom and resourcefulness of Mr Patten. On the other hand, fire gives birth to earth, so the earth element symbolises creativity and intelligence, which Mr Patten apparently possesses in abundance. Additionally, fire means politeness and good manners, so his configuration suggests he is an intelligent, knowledgeable, polite and open-minded gentlemen, with resourceful and creative ideas.

In accordance with the philosophy of elemental balance and harmony explained in previous chapters, the favourable signs for a strong fire person like Mr Patten appear to be water and metal. This is because water, in its quelling of fire, serves to temper his excessive fire energy, while metal, being conquered and melted by fire, adds strength to his birth year. As such, water symbolises Mr Patten's power and authority, and metal his achievements and rewards. Furthermore, the earth element is also fairly favourable as it not only helps to generate metal (the wealth of a fire person) but it also provides a necessary outlet for the excessive fire energy which gives birth to earth. Therefore, the earth element symbolises Mr Patten's aspirations, creativity and intelligence.

With water and metal being his most favourable elements and earth also fairly positive, the remaining two of the five elements – wood and fire – will be unfavourable as they serve to aggravate the excessive fire energy and generate strong competition. To verify this hypothesis, let us examine Mr Patten's career history to see whether the water and metal elements brought him good fortune in the past.

As far as his family background is concerned, the heavenly stem of Mr Patten's month pillar is occupied by a fairly strong earth element, a sign of a reasonably favourable upbringing. It is reported that Mr Patten came from a middle class family in the seaside resort of Cleveleys near Blackpool, where his father was a music publisher. Despite a rather mediocre early life, once he became involved in politics he rose rapidly within the Conservative Party, especially after the age of 28 when he entered a very favourable luck pillar of water and metal. At the age 30 he became the youngest ever Director of Research for the Tories and at 35 was elected M.P. for Bath.

Another breakthrough came at the age of 39 when he moved into another favourable luck pillar of water and metal, again symbolic of power and authority. Indeed, he was appointed Parliamentary Under-Secretary for Northern Ireland in 1983 – a year of strong water. The influence of water and metal in this luck pillar between the ages of 38 and 48 brought him further success in British politics. This culminated in his appointment as Chairman of the Conservative Party in the autumn of 1990, a year when the strong metal influence emerged and Mrs Thatcher stepped down from the Prime Minister's position.

Further evidence of the strong support of water in his life is shown in the appearance of the favourable water sign in the earthly branch of Mr Patten's day pillar. This position normally symbolises a person's spouse and the forceful status of the water element here reveals a high profile wife. Indeed, it is common knowledge that Mrs Lavenda Patten is a barrister of family law, described by the media as an intelligent and engaging woman. On the other hand, to demonstrate the negative influence of the wood element on Mr Patten, we may note his constituency defeat by the Liberal Democrats on 9 April, a day presided over by a strong wood element.

The above analysis serves to show that water and metal bring Mr Patten good luck. As the years 1992 and 1993 were very strong water and metal years, they should have caused Mr Patten to remain under good influence and in high profile. Instead, however, he became embroiled in the political harangue with China, an event which certainly casts doubt on the postulation that water and metal are his favouring elements. A further explanation is necessary here.

As discussed earlier, Mr Patten is a man of strong fire. Water is the destroyer of fire, so, naturally, years of strong water place heavy pressure on a fire person. However, if the fire possesses sufficient strength to shoulder such pressure, the final result will be the achievement of even greater prestige and status. Consequently, the question is whether the fire self-sign is strong enough to resist such a water assault. Normally a fire person born in summertime, like Mr Patten, has the will to resist pressure and should be able to survive the storm, unless there is some weakening factor in his birth hour which is not known to us. Mr Patten's bad luck in early 1993 also seems to have been caused by his movement from the favourable luck pillar of metal to one of wood at the age of 48. As wood suppresses earth (his creativity and aspirations), it certainly fits that he became restricted professionally at this time and was not able to express his will as freely as before. Moreover, the year 1994 (wood over earth) does not bode well for Mr Patten's immediate future. The strong wood presence in this year suggests he may experience further constraints, even crises in his governorship of Hong Kong.

We must note, however, that the analysis only provides information on the personal fortune of the Governor, not on the numerous other factors involved in the Hong Kong dispute. Despite the atmosphere of uncertainty which emerged in Hong Kong in the last quarter of 1992, it is the author's opinion that the Governor, being such a strong fire man will be able to overcome and manipulate the water influence, thus maintaining a high profile. He should not suffer damage or loss as far as his personal fortune is concerned, but one should note that success in the Governor's personal performance does not necessarily mean he can accomplish his reform plans, a consideration which is beyond the scope of this analysis.

To conclude, I would like to offer a forecast for Mr Patten's future in the long-term, beyond 1997. With regard to this, some of his colleagues have expressed worries that Mr Patten's temporary absence from Parliament may cost him a good career in British politics. However, his next luck pillar, beginning at the age of 58, shows the continued presence of the beneficial water element, his symbol of power. Thus, it is more likely that he will make a victorious return to the British Parliament after completing his appointment as Governor of Hong Kong.

John Major's Fire Power

On 27 November 1990, John Major became the youngest British Prime Minister of this century. The press described his sudden rise to power as "meteoric" and "like shot out of a circus cannon". The rapid development of Mr Major's political career and his sudden election to the Prime Minister's position was certainly unusual in British politics. It is therefore interesting to examine how such a speedy road to success was paved for him in the Pillars of Destiny. The following is Mr Major's birth data expressed in pillars.

	Hour	Day	Month	Year
		丙	乙	癸
	?	Fire	Wood	Water
		戌	卯	未
	?	Earth	Wood	Earth

68	58	48	38	28	18	8
戊	己	庚	辛	壬	癸	甲
Fire	Earth	Metal	Metal	Water	Water	Wood
申	酉	戌	亥	子	丑	寅
Metal	Metal	Earth	Water	Water	Earth	Wood

The Pillars of Destiny of John Major

Mr Major's pillars show that he is a fire man born in the spring season when the element of wood is most prosperous. In his three known pillars readers can see the prominence of wood which, in generating fire, provides him with plenty of nourishment and makes him a strong fire person. However, this fire strength requires outlets through which to release its excessive energy. As fire generates earth, the earth element provides this outlet and becomes Mr Major's most favourable sign. On the other hand, wood is the most unwelcome element as it destroys the favourable earth and generates excessive fire to upset the balance of his configuration.

It is easy to test this reading by examining Mr Major's family background and childhood. The month pillar, symbolising his father, is occupied by the unfavourable wood element. This shows that he was not born of a wealthy family and did not receive much support from his father during childhood. In other words, Mr Major is a self-made man. This unfavourable wood influence continued to prevail during his first luck pillar between the ages of 8 and 18. Indeed, it is reported that Mr Major was the son of a part-time sculptor and circus trapeze artist. He grew up in a poor working-class family, had to leave school at the age of 16 and lived on welfare before working on construction sites.

However, Mr Major's next luck pillar shows that he had a change of fortune after the age of 18, when he entered a period of favourable water, earth and metal influences. These influences are still in effect and will continue into the distant future. To a strong fire person, water symbolises power, metal symbolises wealth and earth represents his aspirations and intelligence. Consequently, these are all supportive elements and obviously helped pave Mr Major's way to the top. I understand that he joined the Standard Chartered Bank at a young age, was rapidly promoted and finally elected to Parliament in 1979, a year of strong earth.

Mr Major's rather surprising victory in the General Election was also influenced by the favourable configuration of the date, the 27 November 1990.

Day	Month	Year
丙	丁	庚
Fire	Fire	Metal
申	亥	午
Metal	Water	Fire

The Pillars of Destiny for 27 November 1990

The British Parliamentary election of 1990 can be analysed using the same technique as that used for the 1992 U.S. Presidential election described earlier. As Mr Major is a fire man, the fire that appears both in the month and day of this date symbolise his competitors. In this instance, they were the two opposition candidates, Mr Heseltine and Mr Hurd. However, one of these competing fire elements is sitting on water, so is very weak indeed, while the other is sitting on metal, also a weak configuration for fire. Thus, neither competitors were a match for Mr Major's strong fire and his victory was clearly written in destiny.

I have read that Western astrologers held Mr Major in very high regard and described him as a strong and determined man, yet diplomatic in human relationships. I fully agree with such a character analysis as these are often the positive qualities of a strong fire person. As mentioned in the previous chapter concerning the destiny of Governor Chris Patten, fire also symbolises the warmth of the sun, politeness and openness. Therefore, Mr Major was able to gain popularity with the public after his election. The following Year of the Ram (1991) was a year of metal and earth, favourable elements which enabled him to show his talents and achieve his aspirations.

However, in the Year of the Monkey (1992), his popularity declined rapidly as he encountered a string of problems associated with currency devaluation, the closing down of the coal mines and unification in the E.C. The Monkey is a year of water on metal but, while metal is a favourable element, the strong water on the heavenly stem is a destroyer of fire, exhausting the metal and placing considerable pressure on Mr Major. Being a strong fire person, he was able to withstand a direct attack from water. However, the most dangerous factor is that water will generate more wood which will suppress the favourable earth element in Mr Major's pillars. As earth symbolises his creativity, intelligence and aspirations, its suppression manifests itself as obstacles restraining him from carrying out his ideas and policies.

This is exactly what he encountered in 1992. For example, his plan to close down some of the unproductive coal mines caused a crisis and, under pressure, he had to modify the proposal. In the early part of the year, the water power was not yet at its zenith, so he was able pass his proposals by a very narrow margin. But, with the arrival of strong water in the autumn and winter seasons, Mr Major had to face a string of crisis situations. He eventually survived the stormy economic and political situation of late 1992, thanks to the firm fire power in his destiny.

The year of the Rooster (1993) is yet another year of metal and water. However, the water in 1993 belongs to the *yin* category and is moderate in nature, compared with the strong ocean-like water of 1992. Despite this depressing water influence, the attack on Mr Major's fire will not be as severe. Therefore, if he can survive the great waves of 1992 and 1993, his future should be a lot less turbulent.

Destiny of a General: Norman Schwarzkopf

One of the most popular figures in the U.S. in 1991 was General Norman Schwarzkopf. Under his leadership, the US achieved total victory in the Gulf War, with minimum casualties. The triumph of General Schwarzkopf in early 1991 has led him to be regarded as an American national hero, who restored the country's pride and confidence after the bitter experiences of the Korean and Vietnam Wars.

I have taken a keen interest in studying the pillars of the General and attempted to find his correct birth data when Operation Desert Shield began in late 1990. The media reported that 22 August 1934 was his birthday. This date is expressed in pillars as follows.

Hour	Day	Month	Year
	乙	壬	甲
?	Wood	Water	Wood
	丑	申	戌
?	Earth	Metal	Earth

56	46	36	26	16	6
戊	丁	丙	乙	甲	癸
Earth	Fire	Fire	Wood	Wood	Water
寅	丑	子	亥	戌	酉
Wood	Earth	Water	Water	Earth	Metal

The Pillars of Destiny of General Schwarzkopf

This data shows the General to be a *yin* wood person, born in the autumn month of August. Metal, the destroyer of wood, is most prosperous in the autumn season, so it symbolises conflict and pressure to a wood person. However, in the presence of water, metal does not exert pressure directly on wood. Instead, it will shift its energy to generate water, which in turn provides support and nourishment to wood. This relationship enables a wood person to keep the metal pressure under control. Hence metal becomes a favourable element and may represent status and power to a wood person. This is the kind of configuration we often find in people who wield power and authority. General Schwarzkopf's pillars portray exactly this kind of metal, water and wood relationship. He has very strong water on the heavenly stem of his month pillar which supports the wood. As such, the water element on the month pillar can be regarded as his life-supporter and favouring element. Moreover, on the earthly branch of his month pillar we find prosperous metal which gives birth to water, thus ensuring the continuous supply of water to nourish the wood. Consequently, General Schwarzkopf's pillars rely very much on the prominence of the water and metal elements to maintain an equilibrium.

As metal is in the season in autumn, we can observe a very obvious metal influence on the physical appearance of the General. He is a strong man, over six feet tall, with the nickname "The Bear" and "Storming Norman". He has a definite image of strength, power and determination, obviously brought about by the strong metal in his month pillar. With this in mind, any assumption about his birth hour would make the most appropriate time one of strong metal, namely the hours between 7 a.m. and 9 a.m. This birth hour serves to enhance the metal quality and support his image as a "soldier of steel with an iron fist". Finally, as metal and water are his favourable elements, fire and wood are his enemies as they are in conflict with these auspicious signs.

To verify our hypothesis, let us examine the General's past. Schwarzkopf was the third child of Colonel Schwarzkopf, also a great soldier. Schwarzkopf senior was a cavalry officer in World War I and later a police chief in New Jersey. During World War II, he was a Brigadier General and was subsequently responsible for the training of the Iranian Police Force. Such a solid family background and obvious military tradition is also revealed by the prominent water element in his month pillar, symbolising his father's strong influence. His first luck pillar of metal and water also reflects a favourable childhood.

General Schwarzkopf followed his father's footsteps and was educated at the West Point Army Academy. His colourful career in the army commenced with the outbreak of the Vietnam war, when he served as advisor to the South Vietnamese Armies Airborne Division in 1965. This was a year of wood and fire which became a dark period in the General's life. Particularly during 1965 and 1967, he experienced considerable suffering and bloodshed due to this unfavourable influence. However, at the age of 32 he was being supported by the favourable water of his luck pillar. Consequently, despite the hardship of the Vietnam years, he displayed a bravery and courage which won him three Silver Stars and two Purple Heart medals. Such bravery, assisted by the water and metal elements, is illustrated in his activities during February 1966, a month of wood in a year of strong fire. During this month, General Schwarzkopf led a paratrooper assault on a Vietcong stronghold and was wounded four times. However, he refused to take cover or medical treatment until all his subordinates had retreated to safety. Later, on 28 May 1970, members of his company were trapped in a mine field and the General made his way on foot into the field to rescue them. While escaping, some stepped on mines and died in the vicinity, but he remained miraculously unharmed. Sure enough, the date was one of metal in a year of metal. In addition, the General got married in 1968, again a good year of metal.

The personal history of General Schwarzkopf provides strong evidence that water and metal bring him good luck. This postulation is again proved to be valid by the two fateful years of 1990 and 1991, when he was assigned perhaps the heaviest task of his life: the liberation of Kuwait.

The Year of the Fire Horse of 1990 brought with it the pressure and hardship of Operation Desert Shield. However, as the Fire Horse of 1990 gradually turned into the Year of the Ram (a year of strong metal on earth) all the anxiety, sweat and hardship were rewarded. The favourable metal influence of the year helped him to swiftly crush the Iraqi forces on 27 February, a date of earth in a month of metal. Later, he represented the Allied forces in concluding peace terms with the Iraqi army on 3 March, again a date of metal in a month of metal.

In conclusion, it is interesting to briefly compare the destiny of the General's opponent, Saddam Hussein. Saddam is also a man of wood, but he lacks strong water for support. As such, metal symbolises his enemy and destroyer. General Schwarzkopf, being a person of overwhelming metal qualities, is the natural destroyer of Saddam. Thus, he was the man destined to end Saddam's aggression in the Gulf.

Melissa Rathbun Neally and the Gulf War

Melissa Rathbun Neally was the first U.S. woman soldier to be taken prisoner by Iraqi forces in the Gulf War. When she was released on 4 March 1991, she remarked to the reporters surrounding her, "I am no hero, I just got stuck in the sand." However, the months of January and February 1991 appeared to have been a very dramatic period in Melissa's life. She was not only sent thousands of miles away from home to participate in Operation Desert Shield, but was dramatically captured when her truck got stuck in the desert during the Battle of Khafji. Although it was reported that she received reasonable treatment, her experience

SARA-92

103

during the 32 days in an Iraqi prison camp must have been at least worrying, if not hair-raising. In fact, after the ordeal, offers flooded in from publishers and movie-makers for the rights to her story. Such a dramatic event must somehow be reflected in destiny and it is interesting to examine Miss Neally's pillars to see what elemental configuration brought about her experiences.

Newspapers reported that just a few days after her release on 7 March 1991, Melissa celebrated her 21st birthday. Based on this information her Pillars of Destiny are as follows.

Hour	Day	Month	Year
戊	戊	己	庚
Earth	Earth	Earth	Metal
午	子	卯	戌
Fire	Water	Wood	Earth

61	51	41	31	21	11	1
壬	癸	甲	乙	丙	丁	戊
Water	Water	Wood	Wood	Fire	Fire	Earth
申	酉	戌	亥	子	丑	寅
Metal	Metal	Earth	Water	Water	Earth	Wood

The Pillars of Destiny of Melissa Rathbun Neally

If this birth data is correct, Miss Neally is an earth lady, born in the spring season when wood is most prosperous. As wood is the destroyer of earth and there is no fire in the first three known pillars to support the earth, the configuration presents her as a weak earth person. However, this does not seem to match her strong physique and her occupation as a woman soldier-specialist in the U.S. Army, a career which demands determination and courage. Therefore, I have assigned her a birth hour of noontime, since this hour's configuration of earth over fire would account for her considerable strength. The noon sun will provide Melissa's earth with the missing warmth, nourishment and support. If this assumption is correct, then Miss Neally becomes a strong earth person, requiring metal to release her excessive energy. Fire and earth become unfavourable as they add to the excessive strength and upset the balance of the configuration. Without a sufficient outlet for this excessive influence, her energies and aspirations will be bottled up and she will feel "imprisoned". In general, such a suppression of feelings due to excessive nourishment and support of the day pillar can cause extreme depression and may even result in suicide. Later in this book, my analysis of Elvis's Presley's death and possible suicide gives a more detailed explanation of elemental excess and its effect on the emotions.

For Miss Neally, however, the intensity of the excessive fire and earth elements is comparatively less serious. At the age of 20, she was still in a luck pillar of earth. It was not a prosperous stage in her life as her marriage ended in divorce. Since earth also symbolises colleagues and friends, it was a period most suitable for army life. Then came January 1991, a month of strong earth, further emphasising social interaction as opposed to individual life. This was the month when Melissa had to live with 370,000 U.S. soldiers in the Saudi Arabian desert. Plenty of earth influencing her pillars also reflected her dull life in the sand (earth).

The precise date of Miss Neally's capture is not clear. Some reports said it was 30 January, while others claimed it was 31 January. It appears to me that 30 January, a date of water in a month of earth, is more likely, as the weak water clashed with the fire in Melissa's hour pillar and stimulated adverse effects. Such a conflict also reflects action and activity, and it fits well with the report that Melissa's truck turned over in the sand and Iraqi soldiers fired at her before taking her prisoner. Melissa was shot in the arm and this injury is also shown in the water and fire conflict, fire often symbolising bloodshed. Regardless of this, both 30 and 31 of January were unfavourable dates for her as both had overwhelming earth influences. Hence she was perfectly correct in describing her mishap as getting "stuck in the sand" (earth), as it was earth that caused her downfall.

As the month of earth deprived Melissa of her freedom, we can expect to find her liberation occurring when the earth influence fades away. This took place in February, a month of wood when earth totally lost its power. Readers should also note that Melissa turned 21 in early March 1991. This meant that she left the unfavourable luck pillar of earth and entered a new luck pillar of fire and water, with water dominating. This new phase of life may explain why she was released from imprisonment so quickly. Moreover, as water is an object conquered by earth, the water element symbolises wealth to Melissa. We can expect it to bring her fame, riches and romance in the years to come.

Why Sammy Davis Jr and Jim Hensen Died on the Same Day

Readers have now discovered how much of human life can be revealed through the art of the Four Pillars of Destiny. So far, I have concentrated on analyses of personality, career potentials, fluctuations in personal fortune and on the circumstances of important or tragic events. However, there is yet another, perhaps even more interesting area that the Four Pillars can effectively cover, namely the state of our health. Indeed, traditional Chinese herbal medicine, like the art of the Four Pillars, is founded on the theory of the five basic elements. Chinese medicine emphasises the balance between *yin* and the *yang* within the human body and classifies the internal organs according to the five basic elements. The following is a list of elements with some of the major bodily organs that they represent.

Metal	respiratory organs, skin, intestines
Wood	limbs, neck, blood vessels, head, liver, spinal cord
Water	bones, kidney, sex organs, ear
Fire	blood, heart, brain, nervous system, eyes
Earth	digestive organs, flesh, nose.

Through this symbolism it is possible to translate the elemental configurations of a person's birth data in terms specifically relating to health and fitness. Once we have considered the pillars in this way, it is not difficult to tell which part of the body is the weakest and most susceptible to disease. For example, if the wood element is the weakest in a person's pillars, it means that he or she is more likely to have medical problems associated with the liver or other organs symbolised by that element. Moreover, if the wood element is of paramount importance in the configuration of pillars, or if it plays the role of the life-supporter, maintaining the balance among all other elements, a concentrated attack on it will often lead to death due to liver cancer or some other fatal disease associated with the major organs that wood represents.

The fact that each of the four pillars in a person's birth data has two parts (the heavenly stem and the earthly branch) enables us to pinpoint the problem areas of health with more accuracy. In general, the heavenly stems symbolise the upper parts of the body, usually those above the shoulder, while the earthly branches reflect the lower parts and the internal organs. For example, if a birth configuration shows wood on the heavenly stem being threatened by metal, the subject is susceptible to disease of the neck or head. On the other hand, if the wood in the earthly branch actually clashes with strong metal, it often predicts liver disease, harm to the limbs or surgical operation.

Even more specifically, the art of the Four Pillars allows us to examine the left and right por-

tions of the body separately. When viewing a set of four pillars, the hour and day pillars are on our right, thus symbolising the right portion of the body. By the same token, the month and year pillars are on the left, hence reflecting the health of the left side. An interesting example of this is that people who have a weak fire element on the heavenly stem of the year pillar are often short-sighted, with the left eye being specifically more defective than the right.

We may now illustrate these theories by applying them to the birth data of two famous personalities: the jazz singer and showman, Sammy Davies Jr and the "Muppet" master, Jim Hensen. I have chosen these apparently unconnected celebrities as examples because they in fact have two things in common: they both died of diseases related to the respiratory organs on exactly the same day (16 May 1990). Of course, the layman may dismiss these unifying factors as mere coincidence, but to a firm believer in destiny, nothing can escape the influence of the five basic elements which constitute everything in the universe, including human life. The theory of the Four Pillars can therefore explain and rationalise why these celebrities died on the same day and the similar manner of their deaths.

We know from media coverage that Sammy Davies Jr passed away as a result of throat cancer, while Jim Hensen had contracted pneumonia. Both of these complaints are related to the breathing organs and from the above list it is clear that metal is the element which governs this part of the body. Consequently, metal must be considered the antagonistic and ominous element in both their destinies.

Hour	Day	Month	Year
	丙	戊	乙
?	Fire	Earth	Wood
	寅	子	丑
?	Wood	Water	Earth

The Pillars of Destiny of Sammy Davis Jr

Born on 8 December 1925, the pillars above show that Sammy Davis Jr was a fire person, born in cold winter when the water element is most prosperous. Clearly he needs wood to support his weak fire element. On the other hand, metal is his deadly enemy as it generates more water to extinguish the fire.

Hour	Day	Month	Year
	己	丁	丙
?	Earth	Fire	Fire
	酉	酉	子
?	Metal	Metal	Water

The Pillars of Destiny of Jim Hensen

Jim Hensen was born on 24 September 1936. He was therefore an earth person, born in mid-autumn when the metal element is in its most prosperous phase of the life cycle. As earth generates metal, the strong metal influence in the month of September tends to exhaust the earth energy. Hence Mr Hensen needed the fire element to support his earth sign. Like Sammy Davis Jr, metal is the element he had to avoid as it would weaken his health by drawing away earth energy.

The weakness of both of these destinies is therefore to be found in the metal element which, representative of the breathing organs, shows the area of the body most susceptible to disease. Such disease will become fatal at a time when there is a concentrated metal attack on the pillars. For Mr Davies and Mr Hensen, such a date was destined to be 16 May 1990, expressed in pillars as follows.

Day	Month	Year
辛	辛	庚
Metal	Metal	Metal
巳	巳	午
Fire	Fire	Fire

The Pillars of Destiny for 16 May 1990

As we may observe, this date was a day of metal, in a month of metal, in a year of metal. With such a concerted metal influence, it is not surprising that both gentlemen should die of "metal" diseases. However, this does still not answer the question of why the metal disease occurred in the throat of one man but in the lungs of the other. To explain, readers can see that there is no metal element on the earthly branches of Mr Davis's pillars. The metal invasion was thus external and originated from the configuration of the day. Again, the pillars of the day had no metal element on the earthly branches. However, there were three metal elements on the heavenly stems which consequently caused the attack to be launched on the upper part of the body, specifically the throat. In contrast, Jim Hensen's pillars show heavy metal elements on the earthly branches – the lower part of the body. His lungs were therefore more susceptible to the attack and pneumonia became the destined manner of death.

The Illness of
Dr Sun Yat San
and Governor
Sir Edward Youde

It is by now clear that the Four Pillars of Destiny can be utilised as a tool for detecting physical weaknesses and diagnosing disease. An advanced application of the theory could clearly be used in preventative medicine or even to aid doctors in locating the sources of more complicated and lesser known illnesses. To illustrate this, I have applied the theory to several other famous personalities to show how it can reveal many different types of health problems.

The following set of pillars belongs to Dr Sun Yat San, the father of the Republic of China.

Hour	Day	Month	Year
壬	丁	丁	乙
Water	Fire	Fire	Wood
寅	酉	亥	丑
Wood	Metal	Water	Earth

The Pillars of Destiny of Dr Sun Yat San

Dr Sun was a fire person, born in the cold winter season. Consequently, he needed wood to provide him with nourishment. The wood element in his hour pillar may certainly be regarded as his life-supporter. On the other hand, water, threatening to extinguish his fire, is unfavourable. Similarly, metal, threatening to destroy his life-supporting wood, is his deadly enemy. As wood is shown sitting next to the metal in his hour pillar, it is indeed in a weak position. In view of its significance as the life-supporter of fire, the configuration provides a clear sign of potential disease related to the wood element, which in bodily terms governs the liver. Indeed, in 1925 when he was 61, Dr Sun died of liver cancer. At this time he was in a luck pillar of strong metal which destroyed his life-supporting wood and led to terminal cancer.

Another more recent example of a medical application of the Four Pillars is the case of Sir Edward Youde, the former Governor of Hong Kong.

Hour	Day	Month	Year
壬	己	庚	甲
Water	Earth	Metal	Wood
申	巳	午	子
Metal	Fire	Fire	Water

The Pillars of Destiny of Governor Sir Edward Youde

Sir Edward's pillars show that he was an earth person, born in midsummer when fire is most prosperous. As fire gives birth to earth, Sir Edward was a strong earth person requiring metal to release his excess energy. However, in such a configuration, if fire becomes excessively strong and is unfavourable it will destroy metal, thus restricting the subject's talents. As such, Sir Edward's physical weakness lay in the fire element found in his earthly branches. In medical terms this weakness focuses on the heart, symbolised by fire. The Governor indeed died at the age of 62 in 1986 – a year of strong fire coupled with a personal luck pillar of fire. This concentrated attack by the fire element led to heart trouble and sudden death during a visit to Beijing.

Potential heart trouble and blood pressure problems can be easily read from a set of pillars. Heart trouble may arise either from the excessive strength or weakening of the fire element. To further demonstrate this, let me use another example, this time a famous political figure who is still alive – Mr Wuer Kaixi.

Hour	Day	Month	Year
	丁	甲	戊
?	Fire	Wood	Earth
	巳	寅	申
?	Fire	Wood	Metal

The Pillars of Destiny of Wuer Kaixi

These three pillars show a fire person born in early spring when the wood element is most prosperous. The multiple presence of wood and fire reflect an excessive fuelling of fire by the wood. Consequently, the owner of these three pillars should be suffering from some kind of heart trouble. The pillars belong to the student leader of the Tiananmen Square demonstrations, Mr Wuer Kaixi, who is indeed reported to suffer from a heart complaint.

The White House Health Mystery

On the afternoon of 4 May 1991, President Bush was suddenly struck by fatigue and shortness of breath whilst out jogging. He was rushed by helicopter to the Naval Hospital where he was treated for an "irregular heartbeat". The sudden illness of the President worried the American public until, two days later, the White House physician announced that he was not suffering from heart disease. His irregular heartbeat was said only to be symptomatic of an overactive thyroid gland

and, following treatment, the President's health was described as remarkably robust for his age. In view of this scare, however, we may consider the strengths and weaknesses of Mr Bush's physical condition by examining his Pillars of Destiny from the perspective of health.

Hour	Day	Month	Year		
壬	庚	甲			
?	Water	Metal	Wood		
戌	午	子			
?	Earth	Fire	Water		

79	69	59	49	39	29
戊	丁	丙	乙	甲	癸
Earth	Fire	Fire	Wood	Wood	Water
寅	丑	子	亥	戌	酉
Wood	Earth	Water	Water	Earth	Metal

The Pillars of Destiny of George Bush

As we saw earlier, Mr Bush is a water person, born in the hot summer season of fire in a year of water (1924). As water and fire are antagonistic elements, we can deduce that their conflict in his pillars could be a prominent feature affecting his life and health. The element of fire is associated with the heart and blood circulation, while water symbolises the kidneys, bones and bodily fluids, including the secretion of hormones. Consequently, this clash between fire and water in his pillars renders Mr Bush susceptible to disease connected with the heart (fire) and the hormones (water). In a balanced condition, the effects of water and fire counteract each other and President Bush would enjoy good health. However, as soon as one element becomes excessive, symptoms of disease associated with the weaker element will emerge. For example, if water becomes very strong, sickness in connection with the weaker fire, symbolising the heart and blood, will appear. It seems this may have been the case with President Bush on 4 May 1991. The configuration of this date is as follows.

116

Hour	Day	Month	Year
壬	甲	壬	辛
Water	Wood	Water	Metal
申	戌	辰	未
Metal	Earth	Earth	Earth

The Pillars of Destiny for 4 May 1991

At the age of 67, President Bush was in a luck pillar of water which was already causing an imbalance in favour of the water element. Any further strengthening of water power would upset its tenuous balance with fire, resulting in disorders associated with the heart. Such a situation actually arose at 4.20 p.m. on 4 May 1991, a date which indicated a concentration of the earth, metal and water influences, all of which have exhaustive effects on the fire element. The earth influence on 4 May is referred to as a "Grave of Fire" in Four Pillars terminology and, as the term suggests, is particularly detrimental to the fire element. It was this suppression of fire by the excessive water influence which caused President Bush's irregular heartbeat.

The imbalance between fire and water in President Bush's destiny was only temporary, however, and did not lead to the diagnosis of permanent heart disease. The reason for this is that the President was born in the summer season when the fire element is at its most prosperous phase in the life cycle. Consequently, in the longer term, this strong fire in his month pillar was able to withstand the water attack. Indeed, Mr Bush's heartbeat quickly returned to a normal condition after two days when the overwhelming water effect had passed.

Nevertheless, this was not the end of the White House health saga. At the end of May 1991, another mystery regarding health in the presidential home generated further controversy. It was discovered that the First Lady had also suffered from the same heart trouble 18 months previously and that even the President's dog, Millie, had a similar disease. The coincidence puzzled White House medical experts as the chance of a person contracting such a complaint is extremely rare. In explanation, water contamination was suspected and laboratory tests of water samples were carried out.

From the metaphysical angle there are several means of providing answers to such a mystery. Firstly, as all those concerned lived under the same roof, we could postulate some kind of *feng shui* problem associated with the residence. However, the lack of detail about the history, the interior layout and the directions of the White House precludes any further investigation in this respect and we may only examine the human side of the incident. Having said this, it is believed that since bad *feng shui* ultimately affects the people living in the environment, its influence should also be revealed in the residents' own Pillars of Destiny.

We have already seen that President Bush's pillars reflected a clash between water and fire, causing the hyperactivity of his thyroid gland. Now, let us consider the pillars of the First Lady to see what may be revealed about her physical condition.

Hour	Day	Month	Year
	癸	壬	乙
?	Water	Water	Wood
	亥	午	丑
?	Water	Fire	Earth

70	60	50	40	30
己	戊	丁	丙	乙
Earth	Earth	Fire	Fire	Wood
丑	子	亥	戌	酉
Earth	water	Water	Earth	Metal

The Pillars of Destiny of Barbara Bush

Barbara Bush is a water lady born in mid-summer. If we compare her pillars with those of her husband, rather striking similarities become apparent. Both she and the President were born in the month of June on a date of water. As such, Mrs Bush, like her husband, is also a water person requiring metal for nourishment and support. The earth element generates metal, so it is also a favourable element.

After the age of 60, Mrs Bush was in a luck pillar of earth over water. As earth is the conqueror of water, it represents the husband of a water lady, as well as her status and position. Consequently, the strong earth influence in the last few years, especially in the earth years of 1988 and 1989, meant high status and success for both Mrs Bush and her husband, who became President in 1987. However, after the age of 65 and from the end of 1989, the First Lady moved into a luck pillar of water. The potential for a disease associated with the water element to occur was thereby increased. Bearing in mind that Mrs Bush was born in June, a month of fire in mid-summer, the strong water in this luck pillar posed a threat to the fire in her month pillar. It was this conflicting water-fire configuration that led to the heart complaint so similar to her husband's. Exactly when her disease occurred is not clearly known but some reports said that it was during December 1989, a month of water in a year of fire. As winter is a season when water is most prosperous, the water influence from the First Lady's luck pillar would have been further intensified, again adding to the conflict and resulting health problems.

The likelihood of husband and wife having similar Pillars of Destiny and sharing the same fate is not so rare. The Chinese people refer to this as *yuen* – a mysterious link between two people destined to spend their lives together.

Dick Lee's Musical Career

The application of the Four Pillars of Destiny in the assessment of human fortune has already been shown to have tremendous scope. But one of the most fascinating and popular areas of application involves the evaluation of careers and professions. To use the art of Destiny to identify human potentials and aptitudes enables us to make prosperous choices in life and avoid wasting time and effort in the pursuit of impossible dreams. The philosophy of the Four Pillars of Destiny divides professions into four major groups: those associated with power and status; those associated with money; those related to creativity and talent; and those concerning education, art and academia. In this chapter, I am going to analyse the first three career fields as they are the more interesting and prolific.

Let us begin by examining some of the elemental relationships from the perspective of their career implications. If a metal person encounters the influence of the fire element, fire will destroy and melt metal, meaning pressure and suppression if the metal person is too weak to resist this destructive force. On the other hand, if his metal self is reasonably strong and can manipulate the fire power, fire will be regarded as his status and position. Therefore, people with prominent destructive elements in their pillars are often in professions relating to power and status. Such professions include civil servants, government officials, politicians or high-ranking managers in large organisations. People with less prominent destructive elements are usually ordinary employees of the lower rank.

In my analyses of the destinies of world leaders and politicians, it is easy to find examples of configurations showing strong destructive elements. President Clinton and Chairman Mao Tse-tung are some obvious examples. To further illustrate this point, the following pillars belong to a man of authority and status in Hong Kong.

Hour	Day	Month	Year
	辛	丙	丁
?	Metal	Fire	Fire
	卯	午	丑
?	Wood	Fire	Earth

The Pillars of Destiny of Li Kwan Ha

These pillars show a metal person born in hot summer when fire is most prosperous. There is also a prominence of fire on the heavenly stems. However, fire destroys metal, so this man has great potential in a profession of power and status. Indeed, he is the Commissioner of the Hong Kong Royal Police Force, Mr Li Kwan Ha.

Having established this theory, I must point out that just as there are variations in the strength of destructive elements found in a set of pillars, so there are different rankings in professions and careers within the same field. For example, if the destructive element is weak in relation to the self, then the power and authority wielded by that person is correspondingly weaker. He may hold a deputy's position or be an administrator in a large corporation, depending on the strength of the destructive element and how well it can be manipulated. On the other hand, there are some destiny configurations that display overwhelmingly strong destructive elements but very weak self-signs. In such cases, the weak self is subjected to the pressure of the destructive element and fails to manipulate it. People with such pillars are usually in weak positions in their careers, often working as low-ranking subordinates managed by others. Therefore, readers must note that the prerequisites for careers of power and status are not only strong destructive elements in the birth configuration, but also a self-sign in the day pillar which is strong enough to manipulate these.

Careers connected with money include professions in commerce and industry. In the philosophy of the Four Pillars of Destiny, money is symbolised by the element which the self conquers. For example, if the person is a water man born on a day of water, then his wealth is represented by fire, the element conquered by water. Hence, people with prominent "money" elements in their pillars are naturally suited to entering the commercial field. Consider the following example.

Hour	Day	Month	Year
	癸	丁	癸
?	Water	Fire	Water
	巳	巳	酉
?	Fire	Fire	Metal

The Pillars of Destiny of Sir Piers Jacobs

These pillars show a water man born in summer when fire is most prosperous. Fire is in fact prominent all over his pillars. Since fire is conquered by water, fire becomes his money element, which clearly dominates his destiny. This set of pillars belongs to the former Financial Secretary of Hong Kong, Sir Piers Jacobs.

In earlier chapters I also revealed to readers the pillars of a number of wealthy businessmen whose destinies indeed display extremely strong money elements. Mr Li Ka-shing, for example, is a wood person with very strong earth elements in his pillars. As wood conquers earth, his wealth is symbolised by earth and it is natural that he should have acquired his wealth from a field related to earth, namely the property business.

In the same way as we have assessed the strength of destructive elements in a person's destiny, we can also compare the stability of the money element, to determine how wealthy that person will become. Extremely wealthy people, like Li Ka-shing, usually possess a self-sign in the day pillar that is strong enough to manipulate their money elements. It does not matter how many prominent money elements a set of pillars possesses if the self is too weak to control and manipulate this money. Such configurations of money elements coupled with a weak self-sign is often described as a "poor man living in a rich house".

Often such people have careers which involve regular contact with large amounts of money that do not belong to them. Bank tellers and accounting clerks usually fall into this category. Perhaps our Financial Secretary's pillars also fit with this description as he manages huge sums of money from which he cannot personally benefit.

One more interesting aspect that relates to the money element is that it is often generated from another element called "aspiration". This is defined as the element generated by the self. For example, as Mr Li Ka-shing's wood gives birth to fire, fire becomes the element representing his aspirations. Fire in turn gives birth to earth, the money element. So the element symbolising a person's intelligence, skills and aspirations can generate money.

This leads us to another field of careers, namely people who earn their living from certain skills and talents. The best examples of such people may be drawn from the field of show business. To illustrate my point I have selected Dick Lee, the Singapore-born pop idol as an example. Mr Lee's three known pillars are as follows.

	Hour	Day	Month	Year
	?	癸 Water	丙 Fire	丙 Fire
	?	亥 Water	申 Metal	申 Metal

55	45	35	25	15	5
壬 Water	辛 Metal	庚 Metal	己 Earth	戊 Earth	丁 Fire
寅 Wood	丑 Earth	子 Water	亥 Water	戌 Earth	酉 Metal

The Pillars of Destiny of Dick Lee

Mr Lee is a water man born in the autumn season when metal is most prosperous. To a water person, metal is the mother element and it symbolises food and nourishment. The obvious feature of these

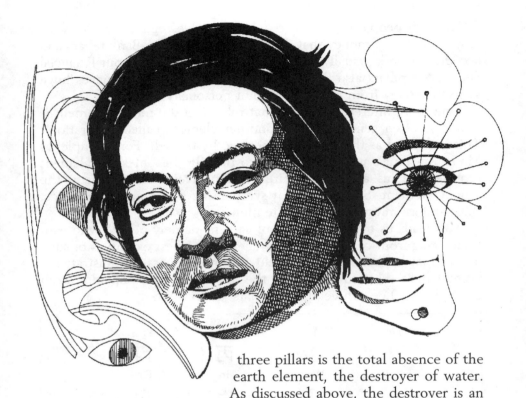

three pillars is the total absence of the earth element, the destroyer of water. As discussed above, the destroyer is an essential element for anyone pursuing a career in power, politics and authority. The lack of the earth element in Mr Lee's pillars shows that he is not a good candidate for a career in politics or big business. Even if he possesses the earth element in his unknown hour pillar, he would still be unsuccessful in this as the earth would be exhausted by the two very strong metal elements in his year and month pillar. The key to Mr Lee's most favourable career path lies in the strong metal elements in his pillars.

These two elements in the year and month pillars can be regarded as the twin "think tanks" of Mr Lee, as they are responsible for his inexhaustible creative ideas and multiple talents. Indeed, at a young age he had already achieved a reputation as a singer, fashion designer, writer and inventor of a unique brand of "Singlish" pop music. On top of this he produced and performed in conceptual pop operas and musicals. However, it takes more than metal resources to make a successful star. A resourceful person must also possess outlets for his talents, otherwise he can only keep his innovative ideas to himself and has no chance to present his talents to the public. The element most needed by a water person to release his feelings and ideas is wood. As water gives birth to wood, wood becomes the symbol of his aspirations and talents. Wood must therefore be the key to Dick Lee's successes in the past years. Moreover, wood is the generator of fire, the symbol of money and achievement to a water person. Consequently, both wood and fire should be Mr Lee's favouring elements. Let us take a look at his history to check this hypothesis.

Dick Lee came from a good family background, shown by the favourable fire in the heavenly stem of his month pillar. His first breakthrough in the field of pop music occurred in 1974, a year of very strong wood, when he joined an agency and got signed as guest artist for TV pop shows. However, his luck pillar between the ages of 15 and 25 was earth, symbolising discipline and pressure, especially connected with school. Education was still his main concern in this period and he studied fashion design for four years at Harrow School of Art in London. In 1984, another year of strong wood, he graduated and became a singer, designer and song-writer in Singapore. In 1987, a year of fire and wood, he set up his own company which handled public relations within the fashion industry. At this time he also worked as a fashion magazine editor. During the period between 1984 and 1990, the wood and fire influences were strong. In these years he achieved great recognition and quickly rose to fame as a talented pop singer. He released many best-selling albums and his success achieved its zenith in 1992 with his own pop musical *Nagraland* being staged in Tokyo, Hong Kong and Southeast Asia. At present, he is under the influence of a luck pillar of water which is again supportive of his favouring wood.

Having placed so much emphasis on the importance of the wood element in Dick Lee's success, it seems to me that his most appropriate birth hour would be the early morning, between about 3 a.m. and 6 a.m. This period would give him a strong hour pillar of wood to enhance his fame and popularity. With this in mind, we may briefly assess his future.

In 1992 Dick Lee got married to his long time partner in musical production, the singer-actress Jacintha Abisheganaden. To evaluate a person's married life, we must look at the earthly branch of the day pillar, the "House of the Spouse". The day pillar of Mr Lee is water on water and these identical elements reflect a harmonious marital relationship, with husband and wife respecting each other and sharing fortunes. This is essential to a successful marriage as it means that partners will share the same interests and be able to walk hand-in-hand though thick and thin in their future together.

Besides singing, Mr Lee also ventured into business and became the co-owner of two clubs in Bugis Street. If he does have strong wood in his hour pillar to support his fire (finances), he has the potential to become rich. However, the years 1992 and 1993 are metal and water years which are detrimental to fire. Consequently, he could be spending heavily rather than making a profit from these ventures. With respect to his singing career, Mr Lee remarked in an interview at the age of 36 that he wished to settle down and have many children. Nevertheless, his current luck pillar from the ages of 35 to 45 is one of strong metal and water, both of which are again very supportive of his show business talents (wood). It thus seems that he will become very active again around 1994 and 1995, when the strong wood influence returns.

The Return of Bjorn Borg

In 1991, the Swedish tennis superstar and Wimbledon Champion, Bjorn Borg, returned to the courts, capturing the attention of the sporting world. However, his defeat in the first round of the Monte Carlo Open by a comparatively unknown player, coupled with the subsequent suicide attempt of his Italian wife, generated great controversy. Many questioned the motives behind his comeback and believed it would only bring disgrace to the hero's glorious past, ruining the image he had earned as the only man to win the Wimbledon title five times.

Whilst still only in his thirties, Bjorn Borg has already lived a very dramatic life, combining considerable glory with disappointments. He left school to take up tennis as a profession at the age of 15 and quickly became the prince of the courts by his early twenties. He subsequently won over 50 international singles titles, including 11 Grand Slam victories, earning him a fortune estimated at U.S.$1.5 billion. Then, in 1983, he suddenly announced his retirement and thereafter his luck simply dried up. It was reported that he ventured into the sportswear business but was a total failure. His company, the Bjorn Borg Design Group, was declared bankrupt in 1989 and during this year he was troubled by financial lawsuits and other scandals, including the sudden death of his secretary. Besides business failure, his personal life was also on the rocks from divorce, remarriage and other romantic affairs. It is certainly interesting to examine the Pillars of Destiny of such a unique person to see how fate gave him such a colourful life in his early years.

Mr Borg was born on 6 June 1956, expressed in pillars as follows.

Hour	Day	Month	Year
乙	甲	甲	丙
Wood	Wood	Wood	Fire
亥	辰	午	申
Water	Earth	Fire	Metal

50	40	30	20	10
己	戊	丁	丙	乙
Earth	Earth	Fire	Fire	Wood
亥	戌	酉	申	未
Water	Earth	Metal	Metal	Earth

The Pillars of Destiny of Bjorn Borg

Mr Borg is a person of *yang* wood born in the summer season when fire is most prosperous. The most prominent feature of the first three known pillars is the two elements of *yang* wood on the heavenly stems. As *yang* wood is often compared to tall trees, such elements give Mr Borg the physique of a strong sportsman and a look of firmness in his oblong-shaped face. The *yang* wood person is often a strong and stubborn character who rarely bends unless he is broken. Such characteristics clearly tally with the sportsman's life and personality.

Although the wood is not in season in summer and there is no water in the three known pillars to give the wood nourishment, the physique of Borg leads me to believe that he must be a very strong wood person with sufficient wood power and water nourishment. Without water, the wood could not flourish as vigorously. Hence, I am assigning him with a birth hour of between 9 p.m and 10 p.m. This is an hour of water and provides the wood enough nourishment to feed his image of strength and determination. His striking blond hair also supports this theory, as strong wood symbolises fibre and hair.

As a strong wood person, Mr Borg's favourite elements must be fire and earth. Fire is generated from wood, so it provides a necessary outlet for the excessive wood energy. It also represents a wood person's fame and intelligence, and it is an essential requirement of anyone with a reputation to keep. On the other hand, earth is something conquered by wood and generated by fire, and it symbolises a wood person's wealth and achievements. Having established this hypothesis, it is easy to see how good fortune came to Mr Borg so early and quickly in life. When he won the Wimbledon Championship for five consecutive years (1976 to 1980) he was indeed under the influence of favourable earth and fire elements in his first two luck pillars. The champion years of 1976 and 1980 were also years of strong earth influence.

Looking at Borg's past in more detail, he entered the luck pillar of earth at the age of 15. This favourable earth influence allowed him to gain great wealth, since earth is conquered by wood. It was at this time that he quit school and turned to professional tennis playing. However, his most favourable luck pillar of fire arrived between the ages of 20 and 25 and this was supported by the fact that the years 1976 to 1980 were consecutive years of fire and earth, helping him to maintain his position at the top of the tennis leagues. However, as we know, the influence of the elements are cyclical. The fire and earth power eventually faded out in 1981, a year of metal. It was in this year that Borg started to taste the bitterness of defeat by losing the Wimbledon title to John McEnroe. He was beaten again by McEnroe two months later in the U.S. Open and it is clear that 1981 marked the demise of Borg's tennis career, under the pressure of strong metal. By 1982, at the age of 26, the fire influence in his luck pillar had completely faded and Borg moved into the unfavourable luck pillar of metal. In addition, 1982 was a year of water which put further pressure on his fire and led him to announce his retirement from the tennis arena.

Arriving at the boundary between two luck pillars often makes for a stage of life when a person feels they have reached a crossroads and must choose between two opposing directions. In Borg's case, it was the choice between tennis and what he called "normal life". The decision to quit was inevitable, however, as the five-year luck pillar of fire had passed and there was no longer any fire power to support his reputation. Hence his movement into the metal luck pillar at 26 forced him out of the tennis world.

The subsequent years, between the ages of 26 and 31, were all under the negative influence of metal, only serving to exhaust Borg's wealth (earth). It would require substantial fire strength before he could expect to regain his former glory. This finally occurred at the age of 31, when Borg left the metal influence behind and entered another luck pillar of fire. Perhaps it was this fire element that rekindled his spirit, while the Fire Horse of 1990 may have added resolution to his decision to make a comeback in this year. He started practicing and training for this as early as August 1990. Despite Borg's failure in many commercial ventures, it is said that he is not the kind of man to be driven by monetary desires. As his motivation comes from fire, representing fame and reputation, his comeback was more likely to have been driven by the need to restore pride after his bitter failures of the past five years.

Regretfully, the fire influence which Borg receives from his luck pillar today is *yin* fire. It cannot generate the heat and glory of his *yang* fire of ten years ago. Furthermore, when he chose to return to tennis in 1991, the Year of the Ram was one of *yin* metal, the same configuration he encountered in 1981 when he lost the Wimbledon title to John McEnroe. Re-entering the tennis arena in such a year was therefore doomed to failure. The subsequent years of 1992 and 1993 are both years of metal and water, which can only cause further harm to Borg's reputation (fire). Consequently, I am pessimistic about his future fortunes, as are many others who believe that Mr Borg will continue to suffer defeat and failure, at least in his sporting career.

The Maradona Story

Diego Maradona, the Argentine football superstar, became the subject of international controversy in March 1991. The Italian Football League announced on 29 of that month that his urine sample, taken after a match on the 17, had tested positive for cocaine. He was subsequently sentenced to 15 months suspension from all football matches, to be enforced world-wide. The heavy penalty saddened his fans and there was fear that it might ruin his glorious football career. The prosecution was somewhat harsh on Maradona and it was reported that he told the press he would retire from football for good, despite talk of an appeal. In reviewing Maradona's destiny we may be able to locate what factors brought him fame and fortune and what is lying ahead for him after such set-backs.

Maradona was born on 30 October 1960 in a Buenos Aires slum. His pillars below show that he is a metal person, born in October when the metal element is most prosperous. There is also a very strong earth element in his month pillar to provide the metal with nourishment. Hence, Maradona is a very strong metal person and does not need further earth or metal influence. This will only bring him competition and conflict. The element he does need is water, generated by metal. This offers an outlet for his excess metal energy, which represents his intelligence and creativity. He also needs wood, which is conquered by strong metal and is symbolic of wealth and achievements. Fire is also positive in representing his fame and status.

	Hour	Day	Month	Year
		辛	丙	庚
	?	Metal	Fire	Metal
		卯	戌	子
	?	Wood	Earth	Water

53	43	33	23	13	3
壬	辛	庚	己	戊	丁
Water	Metal	Metal	Earth	Earth	Fire
辰	卯	寅	丑	子	亥
Earth	Wood	Wood	Earth	Water	Water

The Pillars of Destiny of Diego Maradona

Looking at Maradona's past few luck pillars, it is easy to see that, despite a poor family background portrayed by the weak fire on his month pillar, good fortune came to him at an early age, when the element of water dominated his first and second luck pillars. Indeed, it was reported that at the young age of 9, Maradona had already formed his first football team, called Estrella Roja. They were quickly signed up by the professional team Argentinos Juniors. Very soon, his talents were noticed by the great soccer trainer, Juan Carlos Montes and his skills were professionally polished. In 1979 (a year of fire) when he was still only 19, Maradona led the Argentine team to win the World Youth Cup Championship. He was immediately hired by another football club, Boca Junior, at a fee of one million pounds sterling. In the following years, Maradona continued to remain in the luck pillar of water which enabled him to exhibit his great talents on the world stage and won him the title "Heir of Pele". In 1984, a good year of wood and water (symbolising wealth), the Napoli Football Club paid 13 million U.S. dollars to enrol him. Later, in 1986, a very favourable year of wood and fire, he led the Argentine team to win the World Cup Championship.

Soccer fans will clearly remember Maradona's rather controversial performance in the 1990 World Cup held in Rome. At the age of 29,

Maradona was in a luck pillar of earth which was not a favourable phase in his life. He was not as popular as before but the fire power of the Horse of 1990 was still on his side and he led the Argentine team to the semi-finals. However, the succession of the Fire Horse by the Ram in 1991 was not at all favourable for him as a year of metal over earth could only mean competition and conflicts. The *yin* metal of the Ram would combine with the *yang* fire of Maradona's month pillar and dissolve its fire power. As fire symbolises fame and status, and metal is his competitor, the effect is that of competitors and challengers snatching away his fame and position. Maradona may, after all, have been right in his accusation that someone was trying to damage his reputation.

When the news of Maradona's 15 month suspension from soccer matches was released in March 1991, I forecasted that Maradona's bad fortune would continue. In April, not long after I had published that article in the *Hong Kong Standard*, Maradona was arrested in an apartment near Buenos Aires for possession and distribution of cocaine. He was subsequently indicted on charges of violating narcotics laws and the Argentine Government stripped him of his title of Presidential Advisor and Sports Ambassador. This multiple blow to his position and reputation must have resulted from the suppression of the fire element by its enemies, metal and earth, which featured prominently in the month of April 1991. As this date was a month of water on earth in a year of metal on earth, the single fire element on Maradona's month pillar was defenceless, causing a total loss of status to the footballer.

Immediately after his arrest, the question on everyone's lips was whether the football superstar would be imprisoned. In fact, the answer to such a grave prospect may be found in the techniques of reading "imprisonment" from a person's Pillars of Destiny. Imprisonment can be compared, in an extreme degree, to the bottling up of feelings and energy, without any outlet. For example, Nelson Mandela, the leader of African National Congress, is a strong fire person who needs earth as outlet for his energy. He was jailed in 1962, a year of wood which destroyed his favouring earth element, leaving no outlet for his energy. His luck pillar of wood, between the ages of 44 and 64, kept the earth suppressed and he was only released in 1990, a year of metal over fire. It was then that metal could cut down the wood to nourish fire, which in turn supported earth's release from captivity, rather like removing the cork from the bottle in which he was trapped.

If we apply the same theory to Maradona's pillars, we can clearly see that imprisonment was not in his destiny. If it was, his outlet of metal energy, symbolised by the water element, would have been heavily suppressed by earth. While Maradona was in an earth luck pillar, the years 1992 and 1993 showed no strong earth configuration. To the contrary, his outlet of energy (water) remained firm. As I predicted in the Hong Kong press in May 1991, Maradona could not be sentenced to a lengthy imprisonment. It appeared that the greatest loss to him was his reputation and status, not his freedom. Indeed, with the advent of 1992, a year of strong water, the footballer returned to the soccer scene. This matches well with the postulation that water provides him with the opportunity to display his skills. His new luck pillar of metal and wood after the age of 33 should also bring him greater wealth.

Famous Faces Reflected in Destiny

Yet another fascinating technique of the Four Pillars of Destiny allows us to read a person's facial features and physical appearance in their birth data. Masters of this art can give startlingly accurate descriptions of a person whom they have never met before, simply by considering the elemental configuration of their pillars. Such descriptions can include the shape of the face, nose, eyes, lips and even highlight unusual features such as scars and moles. While this skill seems initially mystifying, it is by no means a psychic phenomenon and, once familiar with the basic laws of the five elements, it is possible for readers to conduct similar exercises themselves.

Earlier we saw that each of the five elements is representative of various parts of the body. In the same way, the shape and characteristics of the human face are influenced by the configuration of the elements in the pillars. To begin with, the general form of the face is determined by the relative strengths and weaknesses of each element in the pillars, together with its symbolic shape. The following list shows how shape is related to each element:

Metal	–	Oval
Wood	–	Triangular
Water	–	Round
Fire	–	Oblong
Earth	–	Square

For example, if a person's pillars show he is a metal man and the strength of this metal is fairly strong, his face will be oval in shape. However, if he was born in winter (when water is most prosperous) and the water element is dominating the four pillars, then he will have a round face.

The key to determining the correct facial shape is to carefully evaluate all elements in the pillars and select the one which is dominating. This element provides the foundation upon which to build up a portrait. Having selected the basic shape, one should then consider the influence of other elements to make any necessary modifications before gradually drawing up the most approximate figure. To demonstrate with an example, the following pillars belong to the popular Hong Kong singer, Anita Mui.

Hour	Day	Month	Year
丁	丙	壬	癸
Fire	Fire	Water	Water
酉	戌	戌	卯
Metal	Earth	Earth	Wood

The Pillars of Destiny of Anita Mui

Miss Mui is a fire person, so her face is basically oblong or rectangular. However, her fire is weak as there are two water elements on the heavenly stems. As the heavenly stems reflect the top half of the body, they naturally have more influence on the face. These two water elements will therefore give Miss Mui's face a touch of roundness. Besides fire and water, readers should also notice the prominent earth elements which, being on the earthly branches, exert a more subtle influence. They serve to slightly square the face and gently emphasise its angular features, particularly her pretty cheek bones.

Having established the shape of the face, we can continue to add other features, such as eyes, nose, ears and mouth. Each of these parts is again symbolised by an element, as follow.

Eyebrows	–	Wood
Eyes	–	Fire, water
Nose, cheeks	–	Earth
Chin	–	Wood
Teeth, skin	–	Metal
Ear, hair	–	Water, wood
Lips	–	Fire

Again, readers should evaluate the strength of each element in the pillars to formulate a complete picture of the face. Applying this to Miss Mui's pillars, her most prominent element should be fire, symbolizing her charming eyes and full lips. However, as the fire sign is weak, one should not postulate domineering or piercing eyes, but rather a softer and sensual look. The earth element is in the season, and emphasises her pretty fleshy cheeks and prominent nose. Wood and metal, on the other hand, are both rather weak in the configuration, symbolising weak eyebrows and small teeth, respectively.

Besides describing general features, this technique further specifies minor facial details, such as small marks, moles or scars. The birth data below provides a good example with which to illustrate this point.

Hour	Day	Month	Year
壬	乙	庚	戊
Water	Wood	Metal	Earth
午	丑	申	戌
Fire	Earth	Metal	Earth

The Pillars of Destiny of Madonna

Madonna, the superstar actress and singer, is a wood person born in early autumn when metal is most prosperous. The most prominent elements in her pillars are metal and earth. From this configuration we

may firstly postulate that, being a *yin* wood person suppressed by strong metal, she should not be very tall. However, the three earth elements provide her with a firm figure, and pretty cheeks and nose. Moreover, as the metal element is both in season and prominent on her heavenly stems, she should have an oval-shaped face, with a slightly sharp or pointed chin due to the wood effect. Strong metal also provides her with healthy teeth and white or fair skin. Like Anita Mui, the weak fire in her configuration suggests sexy eyes.

To add the finishing touches to an obviously pretty face, I can also reveal that Madonna has a mole on the right side of her face. This is reflected in her day pillar of wood sitting on earth. Earth symbolises muscle and wood is the element that destroys earth. Thus, the wood sitting on earth is like a wooden pole piercing a hole through the earth: it leaves a mark, translated as a mole on the face. Indeed, the pretty mole which sits above Madonna's lips has become the trademark of her famous sensuality.

Another example of the correlation between moles and the wood-earth configuration may be seen in the pillars of the British rock singer, David Bowie.

Hour	Day	Month	Year
甲	丁	辛	丙
Wood	Fire	Metal	Fire
辰	亥	丑	戌
Earth	Water	Earth	Earth

The Pillars of Destiny of David Bowie

This set of pillars show a fire person born in cold winter in a month of earth. The day pillar of fire, supported by wood, gives him a long thin face and penetrating eyes. The three earth elements on his earthly branches constitute prominent cheek bones and an attractive nose. However, the metal appearing on the month pillar is not a favourable element as it generates water to threaten the fire. Such an elemental conflict manifests itself in rather unattractive teeth. Nevertheless, if we turn to the hour pillar, Mr Bowie's birth data, like Madonna's, shows the wood-earth configuration. Indeed, a close inspection reveals a small mole on the right above his lips, very similar to the one found on Madonna's face.

If the famous faces of pop seems a trivial subject, we may consider the face of a gentleman who achieved fame for very different reasons. The following set of pillars belong to a man who died some years ago, but whose face is known worldwide.

Hour	Day	Month	Year
甲	丁	甲	癸
Wood	Fire	Wood	Water
辰	酉	子	巳
Earth	Metal	Water	Fire

The Pillars of Destiny of Mao Tse-tung

Perhaps the only link between Chairman Mao Tse-tung and the superstars of pop discussed earlier is that they share the same hour pillar of wood on earth. Sure enough, the hero of the People's Republic of

China had a prominent mole on his chin.

The subject of moles has been extensively covered in another branch of Chinese fortune-telling – the art of face-reading. The Chinese believe that human fortune is not only reflected in birth data, but also in the face. Just as the features of each face are different, so the fortunes of each person differ. A master of this art can tell a person's past and future accurately just by looking at his face.

Each part of the human face represents an area or aspect of human life. For example, the nose of a man symbolises his wealth, the cheeks reflect power and authority, the lips passion and honesty, and the shape of the eyebrows the relationship with brothers and sisters. Different parts of the face also represent different ages and phases of life, allowing face-readers to predict a person's prosperity at different times. For example, a badly shaped ear is often associated with poverty in childhood, as the ears reflect fortune between birth and fourteen years old.

In accordance with the theory of predicting fortune in the face, the Chinese believe facial moles are unlucky signs. Most almanacs give detailed support to the famous Chinese proverb that warns, "No good mole may be found on the face." With very few exceptions, most facial moles are given unpleasant meanings. The following are some common examples:

Moles underneath the eyes, known as "tear moles", usually reflect trouble with children and grandchildren.

140

Moles found in the eyebrows are omens of danger in connection with water. They warn against too much swimming or diving.

Moles found on women's cheeks are said to reflect misfortune to her husband. Sometimes the husband will suffer from liver disease.

Moles found next to the eye on the right mean an unhappy marriage or divorce. Those found on women's throats usually have similar implications.

An exception to these rules is a mole found on the ears. This is taken to mean wisdom, kindness and respect to parents.

One more interesting belief about moles is that they are sometimes found in pairs. If a mole is seen on the face, its partner is usually found on some less obvious part of the body. The following list shows parts of the body which are said to share moles:

Forehead	–	Knees
Ear	–	Buttocks
Eyes	–	Breast
Nose, Lips	–	Sex organs
Between the eyes	–	Chest

As most of the moles on the face have negative implications, it is natural for some Chinese fortune-tellers to advocate their removal. However, it is my opinion that a person's pillars must also be examined before making such a decision. As explained earlier, the mole is a symbol of the wood element in a person's birth data. Consequently, if wood is a favourable and needed element to the subject (for example, if the person is a weak fire sign relying on wood to give nourishment) the mole, representing the wood, could be his life-supporter. As such he cannot afford to remove it and upset the balance of his pillars.

A good example of this was controversially highlighted in the media in 1990, when a prominent Hong Kong figure became the subject of adverse publicity soon after having a facial mole removed by cosmetic surgery. The question arose over whether this lady's exercise of free-will in removing the mole could actually alter her preordained destiny. According to my interpretation of her pillars, the answer is that it could not. The lady was indeed a weak wood person, requiring the wood element for support. Moreover, in 1990, a year of metal, she was also under a luck pillar of metal. This accumulated metal strength launched an attack on her already weak wood sign. The removal of the mole was, in fact, the physical demonstration of what was already predicted in her destiny. The cosmetic surgery only served to weaken her fortune and do more harm than good.

There are many other techniques which masters of the Four Pillars of Destiny can employ to visualise faces from birth data. For example, excessive fire and earth, coupled with a lack of water influence is believed to bring about baldness at an early age, while unfavourable elements on the heavenly stem reflect a scar on the face. There are, of course, many more theories behind the Chinese art of face-reading and the fun to be had with the subject is endless.

The Curse on the Rainier Family

I have so far evaluated the Pillars of Destiny of many prominent figures and celebrities to show readers the close correlation between the pattern of life and birth data. We have seen that the success or failure of a person's life relies both on his innate character and his personal fate revealed in his pillars. Nevertheless, man does not live in this world alone; we are all members of a community. Therefore, a person's destiny must also take into account the influences they receive from their interaction with other people. Such human relationships should also be reflected in the Pillars of Destiny. In fact, the closer and more intimate the relationship, the more vividly the signs appear in the birth data. Consequently, an expert of the art is not only able to read a person's own fortune from a set of four pillars, but can also see in them any special events affecting family or loved ones.

When I was travelling in Europe in 1990, newspapers revealed that yet another tragedy had befallen the royal family of Monaco. This involved the accidental death of Princess Caroline's husband, which renewed public interest in the unfortunate past of the royal family. This latest accident aroused my interest in collecting their birth data and I now think that the Rainier family provide a classic example of how the art of the Four Pillars of Destiny can reveal the connected fates of family members.

The Rainier family preside over the small principality of Monaco and are famous throughout Europe. The late Princess Grace (Grace Kelly) was an ex-Hollywood movie queen who starred in such hits as *High Noon* and *From Here to Eternity*. She won an Oscar for best actress in 1955. Her legendary romance with Prince Rainier III and their glamorous marriage in 1956 caused a stir throughout Europe. Princess Grace later gave birth to three children: Princess Caroline in 1957, Prince Albert in 1958 and Princess Stephanie in 1965.

However, this fairy tale family suffered a grave tragedy on 13 September 1982 when Princess Grace was killed in a terrible car crash. Instead of looking at Grace Kelly's own pillars to explain her accidental death, I am going to examine the birth data of other members of her family, one by one, to see if the tragic loss was reflected in their destinies. Let us look at her husband, Prince Rainier, first.

Hour	Day	Month	Year
	甲	丁	癸
?	Wood	Fire	Water
	辰	巳	亥
?	Earth	Fire	Water

68	58	48	38	28	18
庚	辛	壬	癸	甲	乙
Metal	Metal	Water	Water	Wood	Wood
戌	亥	子	丑	寅	卯
Earth	Water	Water	Earth	Wood	Wood

The Pillars of Destiny of Prince Rainier III

Born on 31 May 1923, Prince Rainier is a weak wood person, since the summer season's prosperous fire element tends to exhaust his wood energy. However, as we are now focusing on Princess Grace, our first step is to establish the element in Rainier's pillars which represents his wife. The wife, as we know, comes in the same category as wealth, being considered an object that the man conquers and acquires. It is therefore symbolised by the element that he destroys. In this case, Prince Rainier's wood destroys earth, so the earth element in his pillars represents Princess Grace.

The nature of this earth element in Rainier's pillars is weak, as it is found right underneath the wood which suppresses it. However, next to the earth there are two fire elements which provide it with support. Therefore, the prosperity and survival of Princess Grace appears to be totally reliant on the elements of fire. Readers may further note that such fire support, although not weak, is subject to the threat of two water elements on the year pillar. Consequently, there exists an innate threat to Princess Grace's life in her husband's birth data. The logic behind this is that once the water elements are intensified, they will put out the fire elements in the month pillar. Hence the earth in the day pillar, symbolising the Princess, will lose its life-support.

Grace Kelly died in 1982 when Prince Rainier was 59 years old and in a luck pillar of metal over water. Sure enough, the metal intensified the water power, which in turn destroyed the fire support required by Grace Kelly's earth. The tragic day eventually came on 13 September 1982, expressed in pillars as follows.

Day	Month	Year
己	己	壬
Earth	Earth	Water
亥	酉	戌
Water	Metal	Earth

The Pillars of Destiny of 13 September 1982

The date fell in the autumn season, when metal and water are most prosperous. Even though there are earth elements on the heavenly stems, the total absence of fire rendered them helpless and they were finally exhausted by the strong metal. The power of water, generated by metal, thereby extinguished Princess Grace's flame of life. Readers can now see how vividly her death is reflected in Prince Rainier's own destiny.

To further explain this phenomenon, we should perhaps consider another Chinese philosophy concerning human relationships. This focuses on the word *yuen*, referring to a mysterious link in destinies which brings two people together. When describing lovers or the marital relationship, there is a Chinese saying that tells how "the *yuen* will link lovers together like a thread, no matter how far apart they are". It is firmly believed that a man and a woman are destined to meet and be lovers if their destiny is linked by the connection called *yuen*. The fact that Princess Grace's tragic fate can be reflected in Prince Rainier's pillars perhaps provides some proof of this. If their destinies are totally separate and independent of each other, how can the fate of the wife be so clearly reflected in the husband's birth data?

The *yuen* relationship is not just confined to husband and wife. It can also exist between parent and child or even friends. In the case of the filial relationship, experts of the art generally agree to the common phenomenon that if the parent's four pillars are lacking in certain element, their child will often possess pillars containing plenty of that needed element. This again suggests the existence of a mysterious link between human destinies.

Applying this to the Rainier family, we may again see that Princess Grace's death is reflected in the pillars of her two daughters, Princess Caroline and Princess Stephanie. The following set of pillars belongs to the youngest daughter, Princess Stephanie.

Hour	Day	Month	Year
	丙	丁	甲
?	Fire	Fire	Wood
	戌	丑	辰
?	Earth	Earth	Earth

The Pillars of Destiny of Princess Stephanie

Stephanie is clearly a weak fire girl, born in the winter season. She needs wood to support her flame. As wood gives birth to fire, it becomes the symbol of her mother. However, her configuration reveals a total absence of water to nourish the wood. On the basis of the three known pillars we can see that Stephanie's wood is weak and vulnerable. It will certainly be in grave danger if she encounters a concerted attack by earth and metal. The only defence to protect wood from metal is fire, as fire can keep the metal under control.

The accident occurred in 1982 when Stephanie was seventeen years old and in the luck pillar of water. The date was one of heavy earth and metal. This strong earth generated a metal attack on the wood, while the water element in her luck pillar reinforced the attack by destroying her only line of defence, namely fire. Her wood therefore had to die on this date, symbolising danger to her mother, Princess Grace.

The eldest daughter, Princess Caroline, possesses the following pillars.

		Month	Year
		辛	丙
		Metal	Fire
		丑	申
		Earth	Metal

...tiny of Princess Caroline

S... ...n winter. Water is logically the symbol
... ... wood. However, there is total absence
... ...pillars, although I cannot rule out the
... ...he unknown hour pillar. Regardless of
... ...th element will render any water on the
... ...This again indicates that the mother is
... ...oncentrated attack by the earth element
... ...n of weak water. When Caroline was
... ...a luck pillar of strong earth, obviously
... ...her. It is not surprising that the tragedy
... ...earth that added further pressure to the
water element.

Princess Caroline also lost her husband in 1990 and it may be interesting to briefly explain this second tragedy in her life. As we already know, the philosophy of the Four Pillars of Destiny regards the husband as the stronger sex. He is therefore represented by the element which destroys a woman's self-sign. As Caroline is a wood person, her husband is represented by metal, which destroys wood. The metal element is excessively strong in the configuration of Caroline's pillars because it is supported by plenty of earth. Readers may remember that the basic principle of the Four Pillars is to maintain harmony and balance among the elements. An excessively strong element is as bad as an excessively weak one, as a person can die of excess strength as well as excess fatigue. Caroline's husband died on 3 October 1990, a date of heavy metal and earth influence. On this date, Caroline was 33 years old and still in the luck pillar of earth, which only added to the excessive strength of the metal. Moreover, the obvious lack of strong water or fire influence meant that the excessive metal energy could not be restrained. Hence, the configuration of overwhelmingly excessive earth and metal strength in 1990 destroyed Caroline's metal and foreshadowed her husband's death.

The Married Life
of Charles
and Diana

Besides showing the close links in destiny that exist between family members, the Four Pillars can offer information about other kinds of human relationships and partnerships. Traditional Chinese culture places great emphasis on marriage and the family, so the analysis of compatible spouses is often one of the most popular areas of the art. Masters apply certain techniques in reading birth data which can reveal the most suitable partner to look for, the success of the marriage and even the general appearance and character of the husband or wife. In this chapter I shall introduce some of the basic methods applied in this area, using

SARA-'92

the royal couple, Prince Charles and Princess Diana, as an example.

The first step most masters make is to evaluate the respective pillars of a couple to see if they are compatible with one another. There are different types of compatibility, but the most common is known as "complementary coupling". This means that the couple can supplement each other's elemental needs. For example, a weak fire man is badly in need of wood for support and nourishment. Therefore, a desirable wife will be one with plenty of wood influence in her pillars to supplement what the husband is lacking. On the other hand, if the same weak fire man meets a lady whose destiny contains a prominence of water, she is likely to be an incompatible wife as her water threatens to extinguish his already weak fire. In tune with this is a theory which considers marital compatibility in terms of producing children. For example, if a man's pillars reflect a weakness in the element symbolising his children, he will often be advised to look for a wife with pillars particularly strong in that element. This belief not only relates to the principle of looking for supportive and harmonious elements in a partner's destiny, but also to the phenomenon of *yuen* explained in the previous chapter.

With these theories in mind, let us now examine the respective pillars of Prince Charles and Princess Diana.

Hour	Day	Month	Year
	癸	癸	戊
?	Water	Water	Earth
	卯	亥	子
?	Wood	Water	Water

58	48	38	28	18
己	戊	丁	丙	乙
Earth	Earth	Fire	Fire	Wood
巳	辰	卯	寅	丑
Fire	Earth	Wood	Wood	Earth

The Pillars of Destiny of Prince Charles

Hour	Day	Month	Year
?	乙	甲	辛
	Wood	Wood	Metal
?	未	午	丑
	Earth	Fire	Earth

42	32	22	12	2
己	戊	丁	丙	乙
Earth	Earth	Fire	Fire	Wood
亥	戌	酉	申	未
Water	Earth	Metal	Metal	Earth

The Pillars of Destiny of Princess Diana

The Prince of Wales is a water person born in winter when the water element is most prosperous. To keep this water from becoming too strong, he needs wood to release the excessive energy and earth to keep the water under control. Fire generates earth, so the elements of wood, fire and earth are favourable to the Prince. On the other hand, the elements of metal and water are his enemies.

The Princess is a wood lady, born in summer when the prosperous summer fire exhausts her wood energy. In her known pillars there are at least two wood elements, two earth elements and one fire element, all of which are all desirable elements to Prince Charles. Therefore, she seems to be a good partner for the Prince.

However, it is also necessary to reverse the analysis and see whether Prince Charles is a suitable partner for Princess Diana. As the Princess is a weak wood person, she needs water for nourishment and support. In the three known pillars of Prince Charles there are at least four water elements, making him appear a desirable husband for the Princess. It thus seems fairly obvious that they are a compatible couple, born to attract to one another and linked by the principle of *yuen*.

Nevertheless, we have so far only analysed one aspect of Charles and Diana's compatibility. We must still consider their married relationship. Readers will remember that the Chinese character at the bottom of the day pillar is called the "House of the Spouse" and is the key to a person's married relationship. Prince Charles's spouse-sign is occupied by a wood element, which is one of his favourable signs. His day pillar of water, symbolising himself, gives nourishment and support to the wood. This reflects that he feels great affection for his wife. However, such love could be excessive, since there are too many water elements surrounding one single wood.

On the other hand, Lady Diana's spouse-sign is unfortunately occupied by an earth element. This is not one of her favouring elements and it is a sign of disharmony. It indicates that the Princess may have feelings of dissatisfaction in her marriage. Furthermore, this earth element is considered a "storage" element for wood, meaning that some wood elements are hidden inside the earth. Being a wood lady, such a configuration is undesirable as it symbolises the sharing of her House of the Spouse with other wood. In other words, she may always feel that there is someone trying to compete with her for her husband's love.

The next and more difficult step to understanding a marriage through the art of the Four Pillars is to evaluate the possible changes that will occur during the passage of time. The compatibility of a couple does not necessarily mean that a good relationship will last forever. It is, like everything else in the universe, still subject to change, whether in circumstance or emotions. A third party may appear to disturb the relationship or there may be shifts in elemental needs with the change of luck pillars and yearly influences.

Prince Charles is a strong water man and his female partner is symbolised by fire. Thus, as long as he is under a strong fire influence, he will not be lacking in female companionship. Such fire influence occurred throughout his luck pillars between the ages of 28 and 48. It was also intensified by years of strong fire, such as 1986, 1987, 1989 and 1990. Such years would have provided the Prince with good opportunities to meet female acquaintances.

Princess Diana's male partner is symbolised by metal. Consequently, years of strong metal influence, like 1990 and 1991, would have encouraged the meeting of new male acquaintances. In such years, a third party may have entered her life and caused some disturbance in her relationship with the Prince.

In addition, we may suppose that Prince Charles was very attracted to Princess Diana's strong earth element when they first got married. However, as he moved into a new luck pillar of strong earth at the age of 48, he may have found himself no longer needing or being attracted to his wife's earth power. Such changes in elemental needs often bring about the common phenomenon of married couples losing interest in each other after a certain period of time.

Another way of analysing marriages is to carefully compare the partners's birth data pillar by pillar. This allows us to see if all four pillars are in harmony and often indicates at what stage a marriage will encounter problems. Putting the Prince and the Princess's pillars to this test, conflict only seems to appear on the earthly branches of the day pillars. Here Prince Charles's wood element is destroying Princess Diana's earth. If we divide a marriage into four stages, with the year pillar indicating the first stage, the day pillar shows that conflict will arise in the third stage of the royal marriage. The hour pillar often indicates the conclusion or final years of a marriage. Unfortunately, Charles and Diana's birth hours are not readily available.

Although Princess Diana is now in an unfavourable luck pillar of earth, the yearly influences of metal and water in 1992 and 1993 helped modify its bad influence. Thus, the tension of the controversy which broke out in the summer of 1992 eased towards the autumn. Nevertheless, the metal and water influence in these two years are not favourable to Prince Charles. In 1992, the strong water of the year extinguished the fire in his luck pillar, bringing about his separation from Diana, officially announced in December of that year. Moreover, in 1993 the Metal Rooster clashed directly with the wood in his House of the Spouse, signalling yet another crisis in his married life.

I cannot offer any accurate predictions about the future of the royal couple due to the absence of their birth hours, which could cast a very different light on their destinies. This particularly applies to Princess Diana, whose wood is so weak in her three known pillars that her birth hour could radically alter the face of her destiny. If no water nourishment is offered by her hour pillar, she would fall into a category of destiny configurations referred to as a "Follow the Leader" formation. This would serve to change her self-sign and reverse her favourite elements. A more detailed explanation of such a unique destiny is found in the discussion of the fate of Mr K. P. Yung.

Pop Partnerships and the Lennon-Macartney Split

The subject of human relationships is both broad and complex. In today's society we are faced with trying to cope not only with married relationships, but also with those that exist with parents, children, business partners, colleagues at work and friends. There are many traditional and popular methods used to evaluate human compatibility in the study of destiny. Some of these are handy and useful, while others are based on misconceptions. I may as well take this opportunity to briefly explain the differences between the techniques usually employed in this area.

The most well-known method in traditional Chinese fortune-telling is to assess human compatibility through astrology, an analysis of the animal signs attributed to people according to their year of birth. The common belief is that animal signs of six years apart are not good partners. Examples are the Mouse and Horse, Tiger and Monkey, Rooster and Rabbit, Dragon and Dog, Cow and Goat, and Snake and Pig. However, this is not a reliable method as the animal signs only refer to the earthly branch of the year of birth. This represents only one eighth of the information contained in a full set of pillars. Animal signs thus provide very limited information about destiny and making judgements from them alone can be very misleading.

In the West, astrology is again the most popular tool for assessing compatibility. Western astrology classifies the twelve sun signs into four categories of elements, namely water, fire, air and earth. Each element comprises three zodiac signs. For instance, Aries, Leo and Sagittarius are the fire signs; Cancer, Pisces, and Scorpio are the water signs; Capricorn, Virgo and Taurus belong to the earth category; and Aquarius, Libra and Gemini are air signs. It is believed that sun signs belonging to the same element will be attracted to one another. According to my personal experience, Western astrology can, to a certain extent, be a useful tool in describing the basic temperament and character of people. Of course, the genuine astrological method is not just based on comparing sun signs, but on analysing complete horoscopes drawn up from the exact location of the stars in the year, month, day, hour and birth location. However, an explanation of this technique is too complicated to fall within the scope of this book.

Of all the techniques used in the art of the Four Pillars of Destiny, the method I employ most is called "complementary coupling", explained in the previous chapter. Readers will remember that this theory is based on the belief that if both people in a partnership possess the elements needed to satisfy each other, there will be some kind of harmonious attraction between them. This theory may be applied to a variety of human relationships and partnerships. To encourage a more detailed understanding of this evaluation of compatibility, I am going to analyse two relationships of legendary status in the music industry: the Lennon-Macartney and Jagger-Richards partnerships.

The success and popularity of Lennon-Macartney songs in the sixties was in itself phenomenal, not to mention the enjoyment they continue to provide even today. The mammoth success of The Beatles relied very much on the compatibility of its two song-writing members, John Lennon and Paul Macartney, while their subsequent break-up can also be attributed to the change in fortune that upset such a compatibility. Let us examine John Lennon's pillars first.

Hour	Day	Month	Year
	乙	丙	庚
?	Wood	Fire	Metal
	酉	戌	辰
?	Metal	Earth	Earth
40	30	20	10
庚	己	戊	丁
Metal	Earth	Earth	Fire
寅	丑	子	亥
Wood	Earth	Water	Water

The Pillars of Destiny of John Lennon

Lennon was a weak wood person born in the autumn season. In autumn wood is so weak that it has no chance of survival. Therefore, his wood had to give up its own property and surrender to the strongest element in his configuration. In this case the dominating element is earth. (This theory of "Follow the Leader", mentioned in the previous chapter, is more fully explained in relation to K. P. Yung whose destiny is discussed later in this book.) Lennon's most favourable elements, then, are earth and fire. His deadly enemies are water and wood which will upset the configuration by bringing his weak wood to life again. It was, in fact, such a revival that actually led to Lennon's assassination on 8 December 1980, a day of wood in a month of water.

As earth and fire are his favourite elements, the theory of compatibility leads us to believe that there should be sufficient earth or fire in Macartney's pillars to bring their partnership to success. Indeed, the following pillars show Macartney to be a weak water person born in the hot summer when fire is the most prosperous element.

156

Hour	Day	Month	Year
	壬	乙	壬
?	Water	Wood	Water
	寅	巳	午
?	Wood	Fire	Fire

66	56	46	36	26	16	6
壬	辛	庚	己	戊	丁	丙
Water	Metal	Metal	Earth	Earth	Fire	Fire
子	亥	戌	酉	申	未	午
Water	Water	Earth	Metal	Metal	Earth	Fire

The Pillars of Destiny of Paul Macartney

It appears that Lennon certainly found a complementary partner in Macartney. This is further emphasised by the fact that, since fire is something that wood creates and generates, Lennon's fire symbolises his aspirations and talents. The strong fire in Macartney thus provided a stimulus to Lennon's creativity and innovative musical ideas.

A successful partnership, however, must be mutually beneficial. Just as Lennon found support in Macartney, the latter should also have found some positive quality in his partner. We have established that Macartney is a weak water person so he needs the support of metal. In this respect, we can see that the metal element is abundant in Lennon's Pillars, meaning that he could satisfy his friend's appetite for metal.

In the analysis of the marriage of Prince Charles and Princess Diana, I introduced the method of judging the various stages of a relationship by comparing each respective pillar. We can now apply the same method to the Lennon-Macartney relationship. By comparing their pillars from right to left we can trace the development of their partnership right through from their initial success to their eventual break-up.

In the beginning, the year pillar of Lennon provided Macartney with strong metal with which to strengthen his weak water. The attraction was instantaneous and mutually beneficial. Perhaps this phase represents the early days, marked by the success of such songs as *A Hard Day's Night*. In the second phase, Macartney's month pillar, showing wood and fire, provided tremendous support to Lennon's fire and earth. However, it seems that here the relationship became rather one-sided as Lennon's month pillar could not provide any metal for his partner's benefit. This may represent the period when Macartney started to feel dissatisfied about the union. It is reported that after the album *Help!* they no longer wrote songs together, although their music continued to be published under their joint names.

It is in the day pillar that the crack in the partnership begins to be seen. The earthly branches show a direct clash between Lennon's metal and Macartney's wood. On the heavenly stems, Macartney's water is one of Lennon's deadly enemies. This final conflict and parting of ways is clearly reflected in the lyrics of the last albums *Abbey Road* and *Let It Be*.

The Rolling Stones's gigantic success in rock music perhaps came second only to The Beatles in the sixties, but the group and its Jagger-Richards song-writing team certainly outlived their rivals. Even today they are still at the helm of rock and roll, making successful concert tours and hit albums. The star singer and front-man of the band, Mick Jagger, is a wood person born at the end of the summer season.

	Hour	Day	Month	Year
		乙	己	癸
	?	Wood	Earth	Water
		酉	未	未
	?	Metal	Earth	Earth

56	46	36	26	16	6
癸	甲	乙	丙	丁	戊
Water	Wood	Wood	Fire	Fire	Earth
丑	寅	卯	辰	巳	午
Earth	Wood	Wood	Earth	Fire	Fire

The Pillars of Destiny of Mick Jagger

Jagger's pillars show that his wood, which is not in season, is also surrounded by earth elements which do not support it. He can be considered a weak wood person, relying on the little water in his year pillar for survival. His favourite element is water, while metal (usually threatening to wood) can here be regarded as favourable as far as it can generate more water to nourish the wood. Therefore, when Jagger was seeking a good blues guitarist to form the band, it was natural that he should be attracted to a man whose destiny contained plenty of metal and water influences. He found such a partner in Keith Richards, his classmate in school.

	Hour	Day	Month	Year
		庚	甲	癸
	?	Metal	Wood	Water
		戌	子	未
	?	Earth	Water	Earth

53	43	33	23	13	3
戊	己	庚	辛	壬	癸
Earth	Earth	Metal	Metal	Water	Water
午	未	申	酉	戌	亥
Fire	Earth	Metal	Metal	Earth	Water

The Pillars of Destiny of Keith Richards

Keith Richards's pillars show that he is a metal person born in cold winter when water is the most prosperous element. This strong winter water tends to exhaust his metal energy and he can be considered a weak metal person, requiring more earth nourishment. Consequently, when he first met Jagger he was instantly attracted to him, due to the prominence of earth in his pillars. Since Richards needs earth nourishment and Jagger requires water as a resource for his energy, the partnership is well-matched and mutually beneficial. The result is that both can derive inexhaustible creativity and energy from the relationship, allowing them to produce a string of successful rock classics.

In contrast to the Lennon-Macartney relationship, the Jagger-Richards tie is longer lasting. As both Jagger and Richards were born in 1943, their year pillars are identical, thus reinforcing each other. This made for a complementary and mutually happy beginning to their rhythm and blues partnership. In the second stage, the month pillar of Richards is strong wood over strong water, totally fulfilling Jagger's need for wood support and water nourishment. In return, Jagger's strong earth in his month pillar provided Richards with the earth nourishment required by weak metal. However, in phase three, signs of disharmony began to appear as the partners' day pillars do not serve each other's needs. Jagger is not offering any earth to Richards, while Richards has no water to give Jagger. Nevertheless, if we also examine their respective luck pillars, it is clear that after the age of 33 Richards has plenty of his own metal and earth, while Jagger has his own wood and water after the age of 36. Consequently, I would conclude that at stage three, they have both become more independent and self-sufficient. In this current stage, neither has a need to derive assistance from the other. Indeed, both Jagger and Richards have produced solo albums recently, although they still continue to tour as a group.

From the above examples readers can clearly see the mechanism used in evaluating professional relationships. Such a technique is commonly used in assessing the compatibility between business partners today. As the main concern in a business venture is profitability, emphasis should not only be placed on personal harmony, but also on the prospective financial fortunes of the partnership. If such financial prosperity does not exist, even the most harmonious relationship will not bring about success in a business venture.

Judge Thomas's Star of Romance

The fifth of October 1991 was a critical date in the career of the newly appointed U.S. Supreme Court Judge, Clarence Thomas. On this date, the Senate debated and voted on the confirmation of his appointment amidst serious charges that the Judge had sexually harassed a female colleague a decade earlier. Judge Thomas finally won the vote, but only by the narrow margin of 52 to 48.

The scandal surrounding Justice Thomas became public when Professor Anita Hill, his former colleague, came forward to accuse him of making unwanted sexual advances to her in 1981. The incident hit headlines all over the world and Thomas's private life was exposed to public scrutiny. The mental anguish he suffered during the hearing caused him to remark that he "would have preferred an assassin's bullet to this kind of living hell." In this chapter I propose to consider the Judge's pillars to see whether such a crisis, caused by his supposed romantic involvement with another person, is reflected in his destiny.

Justice Thomas is an earth person born in the mid-summer month of June when the element of fire is most prosperous. As fire is the mother and the support of earth, we can consider Justice Thomas a strong earth man. His earth strength is further intensified by the presence of two more earth elements on his year and month pillars. However, this means that his earth is too plentiful and actually excessive. As such it symbolises the presence of competitors and enemies in his life and it becomes an unfavourable element. On the other hand, metal and water will help to release his excess earth energy and they represent aspirations, rewards and wealth.

Hour	Day	Month	Year
	己	戊	戊
?	Earth	Earth	Earth
	卯	午	子
?	Wood	Fire	Water

54	44	34	24	14	4
甲	癸	壬	辛	庚	己
Wood	Water	Water	Metal	Metal	Earth
子	亥	戌	酉	申	未
Water	Water	Earth	Metal	Metal	Earth

The Pillars of Destiny of Judge Clarence Thomas

The Judge's personal history proves this postulation. He was born of a poor family and had to live with his grandparents after his father abandoned him. Such poverty and instability in his early years are clearly portrayed in his pillars. The month pillar, representing his father, is occupied by the unfavourable earth element, while his first luck pillar of earth from the age of 4 to 13 also reflected misfortune during childhood. However, as soon as he entered his second luck pillar of metal at the age of 14, his fortune turned. The good metal influence brought him success in college and a career in law. With a strong metal and water influence prevailing from the age of 14 onwards, Judge Thomas triumphed over poverty and racism to achieve high social status as a respected Judge. However, in 1991, at the age of 43, he came under an unfavourable luck pillar of earth. This provided the stage for his ordeal in October of that year.

The year of the Ram (1991) was a year of metal over earth. In general, the metal influence which prevailed was favourable to the Judge, as it was in this year that he was nominated into the U.S. Supreme Court. The unfavourable earth influence in the year did not emerge until October, a month of pure earth. This earth influence, symbolising his enemies and competitors, clearly prepared the ground for a concerted attack on his reputation, launched by his foes.

The controversial allegation of sexual harassment against the Judge eventually reached a head on 15 October 1991, when the U.S. Senators cast their votes to decide whether they should confirm his appointment as Supreme Court Justice. This fateful date is expressed in terms of elements as follows.

Hour	Day	Year
戊	戊	辛
Earth	Earth	Metal
午	戌	未
Fire	Earth	Earth

The Pillars of Destiny for 15 October 1991

The heavy concentration of unfavourable earth on that date demonstrates the strong opposition forces voting against the Judge. Fortunately, his bad luck was merely momentary, as we can see from his destiny that he was moving into his next favourable luck pillar of water. Furthermore, the favourable Year of the Monkey (1992), a year of water and metal, was fast approaching. Consequently, Judge Thomas's reputation survived the date and he may look forward to a bright future in the coming years.

Nevertheless we must still consider whether there was any truth in Professor Hill's allegations and whether any romantic relationship cán be read in Judge Thomas's pillars. Without casting further aspersions on his character after the dust has settled, I would like to point out one special feature in Judge Thomas's destiny. In doing so I must cite the example of Emperor Chien Lung of the Ching Dynasty. Besides being a very capable ruler, this Emperor was also famed for a charm and charisma that was particularly attractive to women. He had a number of romances and his pillars are often quoted in classical books as being a typical example of the destiny of a casanova. The special feature that his destiny displays is that all four earthly branches in his pillars are occupied by what is called a "Star of Romance". Out of the twelve earthly branches in the Four Pillars of Destiny, four of them are regarded as Stars of Romance. People possessing these prominent romance pillars are often attractive to the other sex.

Judge Thomas's destiny bears a striking similarity to that of Emperor Chien Lung as all three known earthly branches are occupied by the same Stars of Romance. These are water (the Mouse), fire (the Horse) and wood (the Rabbit). As his birth hour is unknown, I must stress that his Stars of Romance may not be as prominent as those of the Chinese Emperor. However, the alleged incidents were said to have occurred in 1981 when Judge Thomas was 33 years old in a luck pillar of *yin* metal (the Rooster). This, coincidentally, is the fourth Star of Romance, thus making up a complete set of romance pillars, just like those of the Emperor. With this in mind, the possibility of romance flourishing for the Judge during this period was likely, especially considering the fact that 1981, the Year of the Rooster, was again a year represented by a Star of Romance.

The Mahjong Parlour Murders

On 5 May 1992, Hong Kong experienced the worst robbery in its history. Thieves heavily armed with machine guns and grenades robbed a mahjong parlour in Monkok and brutally murdered two innocent mahjong players at point-blank range. The cold-blooded killings shocked and dismayed the community. Equally startling was the news that the two victims who met their deaths during the incident shared exactly the same birthday. Some may discard this as a mere coincidence, but for those who believe in the art of the Four Pillars of Destiny, it is highly probable that the two victims were brought to the death scene by the same fate. It is interesting to examine this tragic occurrence from the perspective of destiny, not only to consider whether destinies can be shared, but also to determine whether the manner of such a violent death may be read in the pillars.

The three known pillars of the two murder victims show that they were metal men. They were born in the summer season when the fire element is most prosperous. However, fire destroys and melts metal, so they become weak metal men. On the other hand, their most favourable element is earth as this provides their metal with nourishment and strength. As fire is metal's destroyer, it symbolises pressure, danger and misfortune to a metal person. It is not surprising, then, to find that the two men were 36 years old in 1992 and under the dangerous influence of a luck pillar of fire.

Hour	Day	Month	Year
?	辛	辛	丙
	Metal	Metal	Fire
?	巳	卯	申
	Fire	Wood	Metal

27	17	7
甲	癸	壬
Wood	Water	Water
午	巳	辰
Fire	Fire	Earth

The Pillars of Destiny of the Murder Victims

The day of their death may also be expressed in pillars, showing which elements cast their influence on that date.

Day	Month
辛	乙
Metal	Wood
巳	巳
Fire	Fire

The Pillars of Destiny for 5 May 1992

Readers can immediately see the ominous significance of fire which, supported by wood, surrounds the metal element on this date. This strong fire influence in the month, as well as the day, intensified the fire elements already present in the two men's destiny and caused their death.

The above configuration can also reveal more about the circumstances of the murder. The direct cause of death may again be seen in the emphatic presence of the fire element, which can symbolise firearms, bloodshed and the heart. Moreover, as fire is supported by wood, wood contributes indirectly to the killing. Wood is something conquered by metal and it therefore symbolises a metal person's possessions and wealth. Hence the indirect cause of death should be money. Sure enough, the two men were said to have been murdered for being slow in handing over their money and belongings.

Finally, we can comment on the multiple appearance of the metal element both in the pillars of the two victims and on the date of their murder. To a metal person, the metal element symbolises colleagues and friends. This points to the fact that there were other victims sharing the same misfortune. In this way, the art of the Four Pillars is not only able to show the date of death, but also to provide a sketch of the tragic circumstances surrounding it.

King Elvis and his Mysterious Brother

Being an ardent fan of Elvis Presley, it has always been my ambition to write something about the unusual destiny of such a phenomenally successful star. The birth data of Elvis is readily available, but there is one circumstance surrounding his birth that I feel must be clarified before I can be certain about the accuracy of his destiny reading. This concerns the destiny of Elvis's twin brother, Jessie, and why two children, apparently sharing the same birthday and the same Pillars of Destiny, could have such contrasting fates. Without a clear answer to this question, I shelved the analysis of Elvis's destiny, until I came across an interesting book written by Elvis's personal hairstylist which contained the exact birth hour of the twin brothers. Jessie was reported to have been born half an hour before Elvis but died immediately at birth.

Enlightened by this information, I am now firmly convinced that 8 January 1935 is the correct birthday of the King of Rock and Roll. This becomes obvious if we examine Elvis's pillars carefully.

Hour	Day	Month	Year
丙	甲	丁	甲
Fire	Wood	Fire	Wood
寅	申	丑	戌
Wood	Metal	Earth	Earth
39	29	19	9
辛	庚	己	戊
Metal	Metal	Earth	Earth
巳	辰	卯	寅
Fire	Earth	Wood	Wood

The Pillars of Destiny of Elvis Presley

Elvis was a wood person born in the cold winter season when the water element is most prosperous. So, although there is no obvious water in Elvis's pillars, water nourishment is not lacking. What winter wood needs most is fire which provides warmth for its growth, in the same way that trees always turn towards the warm sun in winter. In this respect, Elvis's pillars are quite balanced, as his wood is surrounded by two favourable fire elements that provide necessary warmth. Additionally, like trees, the wood element also needs to stand on firm ground to develop deep roots for stability. Such roots are found in the single wood element on the earthly branch of his hour pillar. This not only allowed his wood to stand firm, but also supported the glow of the winter fire that symbolised his talents and aspirations.

Returning to his twin brother, it is not difficult to see that the tragic death of Jessie was written into Elvis's own pillars. First of all, as Elvis himself is represented by the wood element in his day pillar, Jessie, who was born before him, is symbolised by the wood element in the year pillar. As mentioned above, both these wood elements need to take root in the earthly branch of the hour pillar, but it is clear that while Elvis's wood on the day pillar was right next to the root, Jessie's, on the year pillar, was too distant to link up with it. Consequently, it failed to take root and he was not able to survive.

As Jessie was born half an hour before Elvis, his pillars are exactly the same as those of his brother, except in the hour pillar.

Hour	Day	Month	Year
乙	甲	丁	甲
Wood	Wood	Fire	Wood
丑	申	丑	戌
Earth	Metal	Earth	Earth

The Pillars of Destiny of Jessie Presley

Looking at Jessie's pillars, the reader may see that the much needed fire and wood elements found in Elvis's hour pillar are replaced by weak wood on dry earth. The wood in this set of pillars is totally rootless, explaining why the elder baby failed to survive. The dead wood that appeared in Elvis' pillars is also a sign that the spirit of Jessie might have haunted him, creating a spiritual link between the twin brothers. Indeed, it was said that Elvis frequently visited the grave of his dead brother and claimed that he heard Jessie's voice speaking to him.

Having explained the mystery of his twin brother, let us now closely examine Elvis's pillars to see what kind of elemental configuration placed him on the throne of rock and roll. While the structure of Elvis pillars at first appears to be quite simple and ordinary, his configuration in fact possesses several unique features which tally well with some of the golden principles concerning the destiny of famous people.

Firstly, let us consider the principle explained earlier that "winter wood always turns to greet the sun". Although born in winter, the wood of Elvis's day pillar is encircled by the warmth of two fire elements, representing the winter sun. As wood generates fire, the two fire elements symbolise his talents and aspirations. Such a configuration of favourable fire is particularly suitable for people in the entertainment business, as it reflects a talent and showmanship that may be presented to the public. The second merit found in Elvis's pillars is the wood element located on the earthly branch of his hour pillar. This configuration is technically referred to as a "strong root gathering on the hour pillar" and it serves to enhance the strength of a person by providing him with a firm foundation for personal growth. In summary, then, fire and wood were Elvis's most favourable elements. Finally, if we also look at his luck pillars to examine his immense success in the late 1960s and early 1970s, we may note that a third golden rule of the Four Pillars came into play in his destiny. This is the rule that "metal cuts wood to induce fire".

Elvis came from a very poor family background, reflected by the weak fire element in his month pillar. He spent his adolescence in poverty, as his father had been sentenced to jail in 1938 and his mother was forced to live on welfare subsidies. Such an unhappy childhood was governed by his first luck pillar of earth, covering the years before he turned nineteen. However, his break came in 1954, a year of wood and fire, when he recorded his first hit *That's Alright (Mama)*. It immediately created local sensation and rocketed him to stardom. The following years of 1955, 1956 and 1957 were all years of wood and fire, bringing him immense fame and fortune, with records selling in their millions. His career suffered a temporary set-back in 1958 and 1959 (two years of earth) when he was drafted into the army. However, his string of hits continued to top the charts, the zenith of his success coming after the age of 29 when he entered the luck pillar of metal. It was then that the principle of "metal cutting wood to generate fire" came into play.

While this rule sounds awkward, it is actually quite easy to understand if readers consider its literal meaning. Metal is the symbol of an axe which can cut wood into small pieces. By so doing, it is believed that the wood is able to generate a more vigorous fire. In this way, the metal in Elvis's luck pillar supported the vigour of his favourable fire element and brought him even greater success. It was during this period that Elvis became active in concerts and movie-making, the successful film *That's The Way It Is* being released in 1970. This good fortune also brought about his happy marriage to Priscilla in 1967 and made him a father in 1968.

However, just as the luck pillar of metal between the ages of 29 and 38 brought Elvis's career to its peak, the gradual diminishing of the fire effect in the early 1970s saw it take an equally dramatic nosedive. Priscilla left him in 1972 and he became addicted to various pills and sedatives which caused health problems. Later, in 1977, his private life was brutally exposed in a book written by people close to him, a disloyalty which greatly depressed his spirit. In the same tragic year Elvis's girlfriend, Ginger Arden, found him doubled over on the bathroom floor of his Graceland home. Unable to rouse him, she called for help and Elvis was rushed to hospital, where doctors tried to revive him. He was finally pronounced dead at about 3.30 p.m. on 16 August 1977. While it is reported that an autopsy was performed by his doctor, the report was never released to the public. The cause of death was officially announced as cardiac anhythmia, an erratic heart-beat presumed to have been caused by an accidental overdose of drugs.

At the time, many accepted Elvis's death as an accident. Fifteen years later, however, there is still speculation and controversy concerning the actual circumstances of this much-mourned event. In an article published by *Life* magazine in 1990, Elvis's biographer, Albert Goldman, claimed he had made a mistake in his earlier book which described the superstar's death as an accident. After years of further research and interviews with no less than 600 people, he is now convinced that Elvis actually committed suicide by taking an overdose of drugs. With this controversy still unsettled, a thorough examination of Elvis's pillars may cast further light on the issue.

At this juncture, I must briefly explain how we can judge from a set of pillars whether a person has committed suicide or died due to external factors. According to my past experience and observations, the special feature in the destiny of suicide cases is that the day pillar, representing the self, is too strong and needs outlets through which to release this excess energy. Death will occur when such outlets are lacking or are totally blocked. The pressure comes from within: the person, being too strong, cannot express or release their feelings and they consider suicide to be the only way out. On the other hand, people who die by accident or natural causes are exposed to pressure from without. The day pillar, showing the self, is weak in such cases. The victim dies when the elements representing the destroyer of their self-sign suddenly gather strength and launch a concentrated attack, totally crushing the self. Consequently, if we can determine which of these categories Elvis's birth data describes, we may be able to solve the mystery surrounding his death.

We have already seen that Elvis is a wood person, with the favouring fire element fuelling his creative energy and offering an outlet for his aspirations and talents. Indeed, his greatest success was achieved during years of fire and luck pillars presided over by the configuration of "metal cutting wood to generate fire". However, his great deterioration after the age of 39, when he entered another luck pillar of metal, needs greater consideration. Despite the fact that both of his last luck pillars were metal, the latter was of the *yin* category. Unlike *yang* metal, which is hard and can cut wood easily, *yin* metal is weak, rather like the metal used for jewellery and ornaments. Thus, the *yin* metal appearing in Elvis's luck pillar after the age of 39 was too weak to cut his wood, but could generate water to quell fire. In thus losing the fire outlet for his wood energy, Elvis's self-sign was placed in a vulnerable position. This may explain his depression and possible suicide. In fact, the lack of a proper outlet for one's feelings and aspirations is often cited by experts as a common cause of suicide.

It was reported that Elvis was seriously ill by the fall of 1976. Besides being overweight, his hands and feet were bloated and he had strange blotches and discoloration on his face. His doctors diagnosed an enlarged colon, extensive liver damage and glaucoma. If readers care to review the previous chapters about the relationship between disease and the five elements, one can easily see that Elvis's symptoms were also reflected in the elemental configuration of his pillars. The wood (liver) lost its firm foundation due to a combined attack by metal (colon, intestines), while the much needed fire (the heart) was put out by water (bloated hands and feet).

In conclusion, it may not be wrong to postulate that the blockage of Elvis's energy outlet, coupled with his ill-health in 1977, brought about a deep depression which led to his suicide.

The Robert Maxwell Mystery

Robert Maxwell, the British multi-millionaire publisher, was found dead on 5 November 1991, his body floating at sea near his luxury yacht in the Canary Isles. The official government report attributed his death to a possible heart attack before falling overboard. However, the mysterious circumstances of his death gave rise to some interesting speculations and his family were certainly not convinced that he died of natural causes. Some London newspapers even invited readers to offer possible answers to the riddle.

At the time it seemed three major theories were formulated. Firstly, as the superficial evidence indicated, Mr Maxwell might have died of heart failure and fallen into the sea. Some considered this quite probable as he was an overweight man with a history of heart and lung problems. He was also said to have been under stress from financial insecurity at the time of the incident. Secondly, there was speculation that he was murdered and then pushed into the sea. Supporters of this alleged he had connections with the Israeli Secret Services and was embroiled in some secret activity. Finally, there was the very imaginative theory that Mr Maxwell faked his own death to evade his huge debts. The real Mr Maxwell supposedly vanished into hiding and the body actually belonged to another person. We may test the validity of each of these theories by applying the Four Pillars of Destiny to Mr Maxwell's birth data. In so doing we may be able to discover the true circumstances of his death.

174

Hour	Day	Month	Year
	甲	戊	癸
?	Wood	Earth	Water
	寅	午	亥
?	Wood	Fire	Water

71	61	51	41	31	21
庚	辛	壬	癸	甲	乙
Metal	Metal	Water	Water	Wood	Wood
戌	亥	子	丑	寅	卯
Earth	Water	Water	Earth	Wood	Wood

The Pillars of Destiny of Robert Maxwell

Mr Maxwell was born on 10 June 1923. He is thus a man of wood, born in the summer month of fire. His birth hour is not known, but judging from his huge success since the age 31, when he fell under the influence of the wood and water elements, I am inclined to consider him a weak wood man, relying on water and wood to support his strength and energy. As such, his unfavourable elements are earth and fire. Both are consumers of wood energy and will weaken his abilities and health. Moreover, as fire is the element that symbolises the heart and blood, the possibility of death by heart attack is quite likely, considering fire's negative influence on Mr Maxwell.

Let us also examine the configuration of the date of death to see if it can throw further light on the mystery. It was reported that Mr Maxwell's body was found at about 7 p.m. on 5 November 1991. However, the probable hour of death is quite confusing. Some reports stated that it was 4.45 a.m. because this was the hour he was last heard on board his yacht. Other reports claimed that the extensive wrinkling of the skin suggested the body had been in water for about six hours. This puts the hour of death at around noon. The actual time of death has significant implications but, regardless, both 4.45 a.m. and 12 noon happen to be hours of fire in this case. The complete configuration of the time of death, assuming it was 4.45 a.m on 5 November 1991, is expressed in pillars as follows.

Hour	Day	Month	Year
丙	己	戊	辛
Fire	Earth	Earth	Metal
寅	卯	戌	未
Wood	Wood	Earth	Earth

The Pillars of Destiny for 4.45 a.m. on 5 November 1991

As we can see, the moment of death is dominated by fire and earth elements. Both are unfavourable to Mr Maxwell's health. Fire is related to the heart, while earth suppresses his life-supporting water. Hence death by heart attack is a strong possibility. Death by drowning is unlikely as water is basically a favoured element and supports his life. Finally, there is no strong evidence to support a murder theory. If a murderer was present, there should be strong metal present in the configuration of the date to destroy the wood. This is not the case as the metal element is not particularly strong here. However, I cannot totally rule out this possibility as Mr Maxwell was at the time moving into his next luck pillar of strong metal. This may have already started to cast its influence at the end of 1991 with the Year of the Metal Monkey drawing near.

If the available data is not adequate enough to draw a conclusion, a resourceful expert in Chinese metaphysics will employ another tool: the *I Ching* oracle. This is usually done by tossing three coins to draw up a hexagram, or *kua*, which can be referred to in *The Book of Change*. I did consult the *I Ching* to help answer the question of Mr Maxwell possible murder. The answer appears to be in the negative.

Let me briefly explain the essence of the hexagram that was formed. Firstly, it is obtained by throwing three coins six times. The bottom line, marked "subject", is a line of fire and represents Mr Maxwell himself. To see if there is any clue indicating murder, we have to look for the symbol of a murderer in the hexagram. As water is the destroyer of fire, there should be a very strong and active line of water, reflecting an external threat to Mr Maxwell's fire. However, the water lines in the hexagram are weak and not active. This helps us to rule out the murder possibility.

		Water	___ ___	
Water	___ ___	Earth	_____	
		Metal	___ ___	Object
		Earth	___ ___	
Fire	___ ___	Wood	_____	
Earth	___ ___	Fire	_____	Subject

Kua Showing the Death of Robert Maxwell

Finally, let us examine the possibility of suicide. As explained in the previous chapter about the death of Elvis Presley, a suicidal act is often committed by people with excessively strong day pillars who lack an outlet for their energy. However, the configuration of Mr Maxwell's pillars does not meet such criteria as he is a weak wood person who did not need fire to release his energy. Instead, the prominence of unfavourable earth on the date of death indicates this element played an important role in bringing about the tragedy. As earth is an object conquered by wood, it symbolises money and wealth to Mr Maxwell. There is a proverb in the philosophy of the Pillars of Destiny that says, "Wealth encourages the ghost to attack the body". The word "ghost" here refers to the destroyer of the self, which is metal in Mr Maxwell's case. Earth gives birth to metal, so too much earth will generate more metal to attack the wood. Hence it is quite obvious that, whether he died of a heart attack or at the hands of a murderer, money (earth) is the indirect and real cause of death.

At the age of 68, Mr Maxwell was in a luck pillar of water, which should have been favourable. Hence, there is the slight possibility that he is still alive. However, it is difficult to explore further in this direction as the essential piece of the jigsaw puzzle – the hour of his birth – is missing. The birth hour usually symbolises the final years of life and can provide substantial hints about the manner of death. As it is not known here, I can only make assumptions. In my opinion, if Mr Maxwell was born in an hour of earth or fire (say at about noon), these elements would clash with water and eliminate its favourable effects. He would then be dead today. On the other hand, if he happened to be born in an hour of water, there is a remote chance that he is still alive.

The Tragic Death of K. P. Yung

In January 1991, the Hong Kong entertainment circle was shaken by the tragic death of prominent accountant, K. P. Yung, only 13 days after his much publicised marriage to a TV celebrity. The tragedy was given plenty of coverage in the Chinese press and the details of Mr Yung's birth data were publically released. As Mr Yung's destiny is quite unique, I made an evaluation of his four pillars and released an article in the press. It is worthwhile explaining how such sudden death can be vividly reflected in one's birth data.

Hour	Day	Month	Year
丁	庚	甲	戊
Fire	Metal	Wood	Earth
亥	寅	子	寅
Water	Wood	Water	Wood

44	34	24	14	4
己	戊	丁	丙	乙
Earth	Earth	Fire	Fire	Wood
巳	辰	卯	寅	丑
Fire	Earth	Wood	Wood	Earth

The Pillars of Destiny of K. P. Yung

Mr Yung was a metal person born in the winter season when water is most prosperous. As metal generates water and water consumes metal energy, the metal on his day pillar is very weak. It must rely either on earth or on other metal elements to provide it with nourishment and support. Readers can see that there is only one earth element in his configuration. However, even this earth is surrounded by hostile wood elements which destroy it. Consequently, it is useless to the metal which, symbolising Mr Yung himself, is helpless in the face of the overpowering water and wood configurations.

To understand this in more detail we must explain a special type of destiny which exists in the philosophy of the Four Pillars. This concerns the configuration referred to as a "Follow the Leader" formation. The theory behind this is that if the element on the heavenly stem of the day pillar (representing the individual self) is in an extremely weak position, that element can no longer survive and must totally submit to the leader, namely the strongest element in the set of pillars. Of the celebrities and world leaders whose destinies I have studied, the Beatles singer, John Lennon, and the Chinese leader, Mr Deng Xiao Ping, are perhaps the most famous examples of this type of destiny. Mr K. P. Yung also falls into such a category.

Mr Yung's metal self is so weak that he has to submit to the power of the dominating wood and water elements in his pillars. The rules of the game state that any element that supports the leader will bring good fortune, while unfavourable and threatening elements will stimulate a revival of the original self and lead to an imbalance in the elemental harmony. Such a contravention of the rule will often lead to personal danger or even death.

Such an elemental configuration can be compared to a boy born in poverty who lives in an extremely bad environment and desperate conditions. In his struggle for survival he joins forces with the gangsters of that society, placing his destiny in the hands of the gangster leader. By following the leader's orders, the boy is able to survive and even share his wealth. Whatever brings good fortune to the leader will also benefit the boy. The only condition is that he has to bury his conscience and offer unquestionable obedience to his superior. However, as the boy grows older, he may no longer be as desperate as he was in his youth. He may wish to appease his conscience, stand on his own two feet and break away from the gang. The danger of this situation is obvious: in fulfilling such a desire he must inevitably question the control of the leader, thus putting his own life in danger.

The "Follow the Leader" configuration carries exactly the same implications as this analogy. This may be seen in the pillars of John Lennon, who was a weak wood person surrounded by strong metal. He had to surrender his wood property and submit to the metal element for survival. However, he was shot dead in 1980 when he entered a phase of life that revived his own wood property. Readers may still remember his last hit *Just Like Starting Over* – a title which uncannily fits with the revival attempt made by his wood element just before his death.

Returning to the destiny of K. P. Yung, it is clear that his metal self was forced to surrender to water and wood. These elements therefore brought him good fortune. To a metal person, wood symbolises the things he conquers in life, namely his achievements, his riches and his female partners or wives. Thus, the prominence of wood in Mr Yung's four pillars reflects his substantial wealth, not to mention his four wives.

However, I have already pointed out that a person possessing the "Follow the Leader" configuration usually dies abruptly when he enters a phase of life which revives the original self. Like John Lennon, Mr Yung also met with sudden death at a time when his metal self was gaining a new support that threatened wood power. The Ram of 1991 was a year of strong metal over earth. When Mr Yung died in January, it was a month of pure earth and the metal influence of the Ram was already present. Moreover, at the age of 52, Mr Yung was entering a luck pillar of fire which clashed with the water element in his pillars. All these factors contributed to the revival of his metal self, thereby upsetting the harmony of his pillars and costing him his life. In addition, the date of death (12 January) was a date of water over fire. This conflict between fire and water must have also played a role in causing his death and, considering the fire element's association with the heart and blood, it is not surprising that Mr Yung died of sudden heart failure.

Brandon Lee – Death by Unnatural Causes

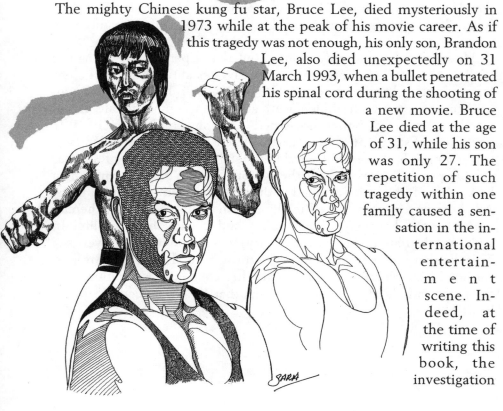

The mighty Chinese kung fu star, Bruce Lee, died mysteriously in 1973 while at the peak of his movie career. As if this tragedy was not enough, his only son, Brandon Lee, also died unexpectedly on 31 March 1993, when a bullet penetrated his spinal cord during the shooting of a new movie. Bruce Lee died at the age of 31, while his son was only 27. The repetition of such tragedy within one family caused a sensation in the international entertainment scene. Indeed, at the time of writing this book, the investigation into Brandon Lee's death was still on-going. The lack of clear facts about the incident has lead to much speculation and there has been talk that the actor was murdered. In answer to this controversy, let us apply the Four Pillars of Destiny to Brandon Lee's birth data.

Brandon Lee was born on 1 February 1965. Like his father, he was also born in a Year of the Dragon.

Hour	Day	Month	Year
?	丙 Fire	丁 Fire	甲 Wood
?	戌 Earth	丑 Earth	辰 Earth
31	21	11	1
辛 Metal	庚 Metal	己 Earth	戊 Earth
巳 Fire	辰 Earth	卯 Wood	寅 Wood

The Pillars of Destiny of Brandon Lee

Brandon Lee's birth data shows that he was born on a day of fire in the winter season. Fire is weak in cold winter and there are also plenty of earth elements in his configuration, thus exhausting his fire power. As a weak fire person, he has to rely on the support of the wood found on the heavenly stem of his year pillar. The fire element in the month pillar is also important in providing necessary warmth. As such, Brandon Lee's most favourable elements are wood and fire.

If we also examine his first two luck pillars before the age of 21, we can see he was under the favourable influence of wood. This indicates that he had a wealthy and comfortable start to life, only natural considering he was the son of a Hollywood superstar. Following this, the years immediately before his death allowed him to achieve his own recognition as an international kung fu star.

Before we examine the death of Brandon Lee, let us also see what his pillars reveal about his father's death in 1973. As we know, the heavenly stem of the month pillar is a symbol of the father. If this element is attacked or suppressed in any way, it reflects misfortune to the father. The heavenly stem on Brandon Lee's month pillar is the weak *yin* fire of winter, relying very much on the support of the wood element in the year pillar. Consequently, if this supporting wood element loses its strength and influence, the fire will be endangered. This is exactly what happened on 20 July 1973 – the date of Bruce Lee's death.

The year 1973 was a year of water on earth and the month of July is earth on earth. The specific day of death was one of metal on earth. This configuration is expressed in pillars as follows.

Day	Month	Year
丁	己	癸
Fire	Earth	Water
巳	未	丑
Fire	Earth	Earth

Pillars of Destiny for 20 July 1973

Each one of these elements in the configuration of the day serves to exhaust fire energy. The worst element is the *yin* earth on the heavenly stem of the month of July. This earth element combined with wood, taking away its support of fire. As such, the fire became defenceless against the water in the year pillar and was extinguished, symbolising the death of Brandon Lee's father.

In the art of The Four Pillars, people who pass away unexpectedly at a young age are often said to die of "unnatural causes". The term is often used in a medical sense, but in destiny study it specifically refers to a death which occurs despite the influence of certain favourable elements present at the time. In other words, that person fails to survive the elemental conflict only by a very narrow margin. If we further examine the unusual death of Brandon Lee, we may see that his destiny can in fact be placed in this category.

The date of Brandon Lee's death was 31 March 1993, expressed in pillars as follows.

184

	Day	Month	Year
	辛	乙	癸
	Metal	Wood	Water
	亥	卯	酉
	Water	Wood	Metal

Pillars of Destiny for 31 March 1993

As explained above, Brandon Lee's favourable elements are wood and fire. His natural enemies are therefore earth, metal and water, all of which threaten the safety of the fire. The configuration of the date of death is full of water and metal elements in the year and day pillars. Although the month is wood, the strong metal influence clashes with the wood and cuts it into pieces. We already know that the *yin* wood element symbolises the neck and spinal cord of the human body. The configuration of *yin* wood being attacked by strong metal on this date thus gives details about the manner of Brandon Lee's death, namely that it involved metal attacking the neck and backbone. It is not surprising, then, to discover that the cause of death was a metal bullet penetrating his spine.

The young actor's luck pillars also reveal more about his tragic destiny. At the age of 27, Brandon was in a luck pillar of earth. Earth is an unfavourable element and does not offer support in times of danger. However, I still feel that he only met his death by a slim chance. The reason is that his next luck pillar is one of metal and fire. Fire is his favourable element, so if he survived the earth influence, the fire in the next luck pillar at the age of 31 would have brought him even greater success. The abrupt termination of his young life at time when good fortune was lying ahead is certainly to be considered "unnatural" and unexpected.

To further explain this type of destiny configuration, I am going to offer a contrasting example. The following pillars belong to a Korean friend of mine who unfortunately died of a heart attack. He passed away on 30 March 1993, just one day before Brandon Lee's death.

185

Hour	Day	Month	Year
戊	丙	癸	壬
Earth	Fire	Water	Water
戌	辰	卯	辰
Earth	Earth	Wood	Earth

48	38	28	18	8
戊	丁	丙	乙	甲
Earth	Fire	Fire	Wood	Wood
申	未	午	巳	辰
Metal	Earth	Fire	Fire	Earth

The Pillars of Destiny of a Korean Friend

Like Brandon Lee, he is a fire person and his configuration is also full of earth elements. He again requires the support of wood and fire, while earth, metal and water are his enemies. His past luck pillars show that he was under the favourable influences of wood and fire prior to the age of 38. Indeed, he graduated from university with a first class honours degree and acquired a scholarship to pursue further study in law. After this he immediately achieved business success when he became the owner and managing director of an international ship broking firm. Unfortunately, he died on 30 March 1993 due to a sudden heart attack.

Day	Month	Year
庚	乙	癸
Metal	Wood	Water
戌	卯	酉
Earth	Wood	Metal

Pillars of Destiny for 30 March 1993

The configuration of this date is very similar to that of Brandon Lee's death. It is also full of metal and earth, with metal in conflict with wood. The destruction of wood – his life-supporter in the month pillar – caused his fire to be extinguished. His heart, symbolised by the fire element, stopped on this date.

However, the point is that the death of my Korean friend is different from that of Brandon Lee's in one important respect: my friend died of "natural causes". The reason is because, at the age of 41, he would have left the luck pillar of fire and entered one of unfavourable earth. Thereafter, his subsequent luck pillars are all of metal and earth, which are again unhelpful. All his favourable wood and fire luck had expired, so his path of fortune would only have descended, even if he could have survived the conflict of 1993. The difference between his destiny and the bright future of Brandon Lee is quite clear.

The Assassination of Rajiv Gandhi

On 21 May 1991, a violent and deafening explosion rocked the town of Sriperumpudur, 40 kilometres from the city of Madras in southern India. The explosion instantly killed the national election candidate and former Prime Minister, Rajiv Gandhi. As I am not familiar with the politics and history of India, I will leave historians and journalists to analyse the reasons behind the assassination and its impact on the country. However, for research on human destiny, the violent death of Mr Gandhi provides a real example of the abrupt termination to a short but eventful life. An examination of his pillars may show how fate suddenly ended this great man's life and how such misfortune is written in destiny from the moment of birth.

During my analysis of Mr Gandhi's fate, I discovered a startling similarity between his pillars and those of the late President John F. Kennedy who was assassinated in 1963. This discovery helped me to formulate a theory for reading violent death in a person's birth data. First, let us examine Mr Gandhi's three known pillars.

Hour	Day	Month	Year
	丙	壬	甲
?	Fire	Water	Wood
	辰	申	申
?	Earth	Metal	Metal

47	37	27	17	7
丁	丙	乙	甲	癸
Fire	Fire	Wood	Wood	Water
丑	子	亥	戌	酉
Earth	Water	Water	Earth	Metal

The Pillars of Destiny of Rajiv Gandhi

Mr Gandhi was born on 20 August 1944. He was a fire person born in the month of August when metal is most prosperous. As such, he can be regarded as a weak fire man, requiring more fire and wood to nourish and support his self-sign. The element of water is actually a two-bladed sword, symbolising power and status. It can be a favourable element as long as it can support and generate wood. However, it will extinguish the weak fire if it gets out of control, for example in a situation when wood is weak or totally absent. On the other hand, metal and earth are Mr Gandhi's deadly enemies because they destroy wood and exhaust his fire energy.

It is easy to verify the above hypothesis by randomly picking some eventful years in Mr Gandhi's history. For example, in 1984 he succeeded his mother's position as Prime Minister of India, winning an unprecedented majority in the election. This was a year of wood which put him in high profile. However, in late 1987, when the fire influence was fading and strong earth was taking over, he was accused of corruption. He was ousted from the Prime Minister's position in 1988, a year of strong earth. Apparently, the revival of fire power in 1990, the Year of the Fire Horse, provided him with the drive and enthusiasm to make a comeback in the 1991 election. However, this fire power was short-lived and, as the Year of the Ram (metal and earth) approached, Mr Gandhi entered a dangerous phase of life.

At the age of 46, Mr Gandhi was in a luck pillar of water. Water symbolises power and status to a fire person and is favourable as long as there is strong wood to support the fire. However, in a year of strong metal and earth influence, any wood element would be suppressed by metal. Thus Mr Gandhi, being a weak fire person, was in an unstable position, lacking strong wood support. The danger of water getting out of control and extinguishing his weak fire was already looming.

This was exactly what happened on 21 May 1991. When expressed in terms of elements, this date is a day of metal in a month of water, in a year of metal over earth. The onslaught of overwhelming metal and water influence totally destroyed Mr Gandhi's life-supporting wood, and put out his flame of life. Thus, the combination of elements in Mr Gandhi's luck pillar and in the date of his assassination made his death inevitable.

However, while it is now clear that death can be read in the pillars, there remains the question of why this death should have been so violent. In the following chapter, I am going to demonstrate to readers how the Four Pillars of Destiny can also predict violent death, taking both Mr Gandhi and President J. F. Kennedy as examples.

The J. F. K.
Assassination

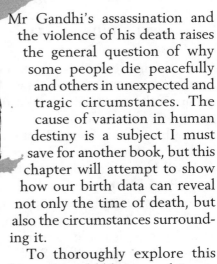

Mr Gandhi's assassination and the violence of his death raises the general question of why some people die peacefully and others in unexpected and tragic circumstances. The cause of variation in human destiny is a subject I must save for another book, but this chapter will attempt to show how our birth data can reveal not only the time of death, but also the circumstances surrounding it.

To thoroughly explore this theory I would like to explain another example of violent death by political assassination. This concerns the famous and controversial murder of President John F. Kennedy who, like Mr Gandhi, was only 46 years old and at the peak of his political career when he died.

Hour	Day	Month	Year
	辛	乙	丁
?	Metal	Wood	Fire
	未	巳	巳
?	Earth	Fire	Fire
38	28	18	8
辛	壬	癸	甲
Metal	Water	Water	Wood
丑	寅	卯	辰
Earth	Wood	Wood	Earth

The Pillars of Destiny of John F. Kennedy

President Kennedy's pillars show that he was a metal person born in the summer month of May. The most prominent feature of his pillars is the strong element of fire, the destroyer of metal. Whether fire can cast its destructive influence very much depends on the strength of the self-sign. To a metal person fire can symbolise power and status if he is strong enough to manipulate it. On the other hand, fire will become suppressive if it is allowed to get out of control.

In President Kennedy's three known pillars, readers can see that fire is not only strong because it is "in season" in the summer month, but also because it appears several times in the year and month pillars. The strong fire is also able to recruit support from wood on the heavenly stem of the month pillar. Such a configuration of strong fire in President Kennedy's destiny obviously reflects a man of innate power and status. All he needs is some method of manipulating the fire power to keep it under control. For a metal person, this can be derived from three sources. Earth is the mother of metal and is a natural supporter, representing nourishment and strength. In the presence of earth, the fire energy will begin to generate earth, hence indirectly supporting metal by giving birth to earth. With earth as the mediator, a metal person can control fire. Readers can also see that if earth is absent or under the suppression of wood, the fire will directly attack metal and put it in danger. Besides using earth as a support to manipulate fire, metal (symbolising colleagues and friends) is also favourable. Finally, water, which is generated by metal and keeps fire under control, symbolises the metal person's intelligence and creativity. He must possess these to manipulate the fire power. In contrast, his deadly enemy is wood, which generates excessive fire and destroys earth, the metal-supporter. In this way the water element can be a two-bladed sword. It can control fire, but can also support wood, which in turn generates more fire to threaten the President's well-being.

With this in mind, it is not difficult to see how President Kennedy was elected the youngest U.S. President in 1960. It was a year of metal over water, when the President was 43 years old and in a luck pillar of metal over earth, all of which are favourable elements. This information can be used to explain, from a metaphysical angle, the forces behind President Kennedy's political successes and failures. However, his political career is not the real concern of this chapter. Our interest lies rather with the circumstances of his tragic death on 22 November 1963. This was a year of wood, the strength of which was greatly intensified by a month of water. It was, then, a dangerous phase in the President's life as his enemy (wood) suddenly became active. Wood can stimulate the strength of fire and suppress earth, causing great harm to his metal self. This eventually happened at about 12.30 p.m. on the 22 November, an hour of blazing noon fire on a day of fire.

The shooting of President Kennedy bears some similarity to the more recent assassination of Rajiv Gandhi. Both died in their prime and at the hand of an assassin. Comparing the birth data of these two leaders, there is one unique feature in their pillars which seems to be linked with violent death. Experts of the art call it a "besieged configuration". The essence of this theory is that the earthly branches of the month and day pillars constitute the destroyer of the self. In simpler terms, such a configuration of pillars shows the self standing on its own destroyer. Such a destiny is like a time-bomb which will go off when the right elemental stimulant arrives. In the case of President Kennedy (a metal person) the earthly branches of the month and day pillars are indeed occupied by fire, the destroyer of metal. Similarly, Mr. Gandhi's fire is standing on water, its destroyer.

Finding an Explanation for Ghosts

I always emphasise that the study of *feng shui* and the Four Pillars of Destiny has nothing to do with religion or the supernatural. However, as experts practising *feng shui* are often entrusted with the task of improving living environments, they are more likely to visit houses which are said to be "problematic". In other words, their chances of encountering supernatural beings or occurrences are comparatively higher than ordinary people. As such, most *feng shui* experts have strange experiences or paranormal encounters to tell of.

I myself have never seen a ghost appearing in physical form, but in my experiences as a *feng shui* practitioner I have seen houses which are believed to be haunted and I have encountered happenings which cannot be explained in a rational manner. Moreover, as I have a number of friends in the *feng shui* profession, every now and then I hear weird first-hand accounts of encounters with the supernatural. Some of these experiences are thought-provoking and worth recording, if only as reference for future research into the field. The following is one such example and describes the experiences of a professional *feng shui* practitioner in Hong Kong. Through his chilling experiences, I also gained insight into the kind of people susceptible to encounters with ghosts.

Before embarking on this account, readers should be reminded that *feng shui* experts are ordinary human beings and, like everybody else, are subject to the influences of destiny which can cause misfortune to befall them. In 1990, my friend was in such a stage of his fortune cycle. Traditionally, the Chinese believe that people who are experiencing bad luck are more susceptible to encounters with ghosts. This saying certainly seems to be true in my friend's case.

His first encounter occurred in January 1990, when he was asked to perform a *feng shui* evaluation on a mansion in Kowloon. It was a new building with bad *feng shui* and he soon found out that a tragic accident had actually taken place at the front entrance only a year earlier. A young child had been caught in the electric gate and crushed to death. After finishing his *feng shui* inspection, my friend felt an acute pain in his stomach. He was rushed to hospital where he was admitted to casualty. Doctors performed various tests on him but could still not diagnose the mysterious pain. The date was 7 January 1990, a day of water on metal.

The piercing pain continued on and off for about four days and even the strongest medication was useless. Then my friend consulted the bible of all traditional Chinese families: the Chinese almanac called the *Tung Sing*. There is a section in this book advising remedies for strange illnesses according to the date when one contracts the disease. The following description was found for the date of "water on metal":

"Illness commencing on a date of water on metal is caused by upsetting a water spirit or the ghost of a child in the south-west. The symptoms are headaches, frequent and urgent diarrhoea and stomach pain. Pray to the south-west with money, water, rice, wine, fruit and candles ... to cure the disease."

My friend immediately followed these instructions and prayed to the south-west. Miraculously his stomach pain ceased.

Nevertheless, on 24 February 1990, a date of pure metal, my friend was invited to evaluate the *feng shui* of a large house in an outlying island of Hong Kong. It was a grand old three-storey building with only one occupant. My friend, accompanied by the owner of the house, arrived at the front door just before noon. There was no one inside. The owner inserted his key into the keyhole but the door simply refused to open. The owner was certain that it was the right key and could not understand why it failed to turn. After attempting for about half an hour, the key suddenly worked and the door opened at exactly twelve noon. The timing is alarming to an experienced *feng*

195

shui practitioner as it could imply that some mysterious force had been struggling to bar his entry to the house. Such a dark force was not able to withstand the power of the blazing midday sun and gave way at exactly twelve o'clock.

However, as soon as the door opened my friend felt dizzy and the familiar stomach pain that had attacked him several weeks ago suddenly returned. He was again hospitalised and during the following five days doctors made vain attempts to locate the origin of the pain. All medical reports showed good health, but the clear symptoms were that he felt a large hard lump in his stomach and he had no appetite for food. In addition, the stomach pain became acute in the middle of the night. One very strange phenomenon which puzzled his doctors was that when inserting a gastroscope into his stomach to inspect the interior, it could not be pulled out. It was as if the intestines had become entangled with it.

Even the *Tung Sing* did not help this time. My friend's father was very worried and he consulted a psychic medium in order to communicate with his dead ancestors. It was revealed to him that there were eight ghosts inside his son's body, of which six were male and two were female. The only panacea was to perform certain Buddhist rituals in a temple. Thankfully, my poor friend was eventually cured after this ceremony had been conducted.

I shall not go into details about the process of exorcism, as this is not my area of expertise. However, one thing I found very interesting about this incident is its association with my friend's four pillars. I have already mentioned the common belief among the Chinese that one is susceptible to supernatural encounters if one is at the bottom of the cycle of fortune. My friend's case seems to prove this ancient wisdom. His pillars show he is a wood person born in the winter season when the prosperous water is able to provide his wood with nourishment. However, we can clearly see that his wood is surrounded by metal elements which threaten to destroy it. He is thus a rather weak wood person, relying on the water element in his month pillar to support his life.

Readers can count four metal elements in this set of pillars. The configuration of the Year of the Horse (1990) was metal over fire. In addition, at the time my friend had just turned 38 years of age and entered a luck pillar of fire over metal. The ghostly events happened on a day of metal on metal. Consequently, all these factors amalgamate to show eight metal elements surrounding his weak wood. It is thus besieged and its safety is threatened.

Hour	Day	Month	Year		
甲	乙	庚	辛		
Wood	Wood	Metal	Metal		
申	酉	子	卯		
Metal	Metal	Water	Wood		
58	48	38	28	18	8
甲	乙	丙	丁	戊	己
Wood	Wood	Fire	Fire	Earth	Earth
午	未	申	酉	戌	亥
Fire	Earth	Metal	Metal	Earth	Water

The Pillars of Destiny of a *Feng Shui* Expert

To add to the disaster, the severe fire element in the Year of the Horse clashed with the favourable water in his month pillar and very much weakened this life-supporter. Hence, his four pillars, coupled with the configuration of the year and the date, actually reflected a very critical situation and one which was conducive to a supernatural experience, according to traditional belief.

The number of ghosts revealed by the psychic medium was eight. This matches exactly with the total number of unfavourable metal elements found in my friend's pillars, his luck pillar and the configuration of the year and the date of the encounter. Even more startling is that the medium claimed six of the supernatural beings were female and two were male, which again exactly coincides with the number of *yin* (female) and *yang* (male) metal elements found in the configurations.

From the academic angle, I think this case is able to provide some hints about the mysterious link between human beings and the supernatural. The number of ghosts matched exactly with the number of unfavourable metal elements appearing in the person's preordained pillars. Does this suggest that ghosts are something which exist in our destiny from birth, emerging to make trouble only when one arrives at an extremely weak stage in the cycle of fortune? If this is the case, perhaps ghosts are not external beings but something generated from deep within our minds.

With respect to this, I recently came across an interesting book which recorded an experiment on haunting conducted by a group of Canadian scientists. These scientists made an attempt to create a ghost. They invented the story of a fictitious nobleman of the eighteenth century and then held daily gatherings in a house. Each participant sat quietly and concentrated his thoughts on this imaginary nobleman. The group held such gatherings continuously for six months but nothing happened. Then one of them suggested changing the rendezvous into a casual meeting. They continued to meet in the house but instead of meditating on the nobleman, they simply chatted. Nevertheless, every member had the story of the nobleman alive in their subconscious. After a while, strange things began to happen in the house and finally a poltergeist appeared. This being was able to communicate with the scientists by making noises and its answers to their questions matched very well the identity of the nobleman created in their imaginations. Such a remarkable finding received much publicity and it is said that Canadian TV made a documentary of the event.

This stimulating experiment does not seem so far-fetched when we compare it to the mysterious practice of the Boxers, a group of warriors living at the end of the Ching Dynasty. By performing certain rituals, the Boxers claimed that they could get the legendary monkey king to enter their bodies, enabling them to fight as fiercely as a monkey without getting hurt. The monkey king was only a fictional figure and did not really exist in history. It lived only in the imagination of the Boxers. Both the practice of the Boxers and the Canadian scientists' experiment indicate that supernatural beings may exist in our psychological make-up, rather than as uncontrollable external forces.

In conclusion, to make some bold and imaginative postulations based on the ghostly experiences of my friend, it seems to me that ghosts may be, by nature, a group of unfavourable elements which affect the elemental influences under which we were born. Alternatively, they could be weaknesses within our bodies and minds, again written in our birth data. When thought of in this way, they become internalised, causing trouble only when circumstances are most unfavourable and stressful to the person at hand.

APPENDIX 1

Feng Shui Charts for Age of Seven Buildings

The 16 charts which follow show the *feng shui* flying star distributions for Age of Seven buildings (building completed between 1984 and 2003 inclusive). The following are brief guidelines for using these charts:

1. Find out the accurate direction of the building by means of a *lo pan*.
2. Mark down the Chinese characters taken from the *lo pan* and check their English equivalents from the simplified *lo pan* in Fig. A.
3. Then find the chart applicable to buildings of that direction in this Appendix.

Example

By standing facing the front of a house, holding the *lo pan* horizontally, the magnetic needle points to a direction indicated by the Chinese characters 丁 and 癸 . This means the back of the building is facing the direction 丁 and the front is facing the direction 癸 . From the *lo pan* in Fig. A, we can see that 丁 is S2 and 癸 is N2. The applicable *feng shui* chart for such a building is therefore S2-N2, meaning a building with its back facing the S2 direction and its front facing the N2 direction.

Please refer to the first part of this book for detailed interpretations of the numbers on the charts. Note that these charts are applicable to Age of Seven buildings only.

Fig. A The *lo pan* showing the Twenty-four Mountains

S		
3 2	7 7	5 9
6	**2**	**4**
4 1	2 3	9 5
5	**7**	**9**
8 6	6 8	1 4
1	**3**	**8**

S1-N1

S		
1 4	6 8	8 6
6	**2**	**4**
9 5	2 3	4 1
5	**7**	**9**
5 9	7 7	3 2
1	**3**	**8**

S-N, S2-N2

S

5 9	9 5	7 7
6	**2**	**4**
6 8	4 1	2 3
5	**7**	**9**
1 4	8 6	3 2
1	**3**	**8**

SW1-NE1

S

3 2	8 6	1 4
6	**2**	**4**
2 3	4 1	6 8
5	**7**	**9**
7 7	9 5	5 9
1	**3**	**8**

SW-NE, SW2-NE2

S

8 4	4 9	6 2
6	**2**	**4**
7 3	9 5	2 7
5	**7**	**9**
3 8	5 1	1 6
1	**3**	**8**

W1-E1

S

1 6	5 1	3 8
6	**2**	**4**
2 7	9 5	7 3
5	**7**	**9**
6 2	4 9	8 4
1	**3**	**8**

W-E, W2-E2

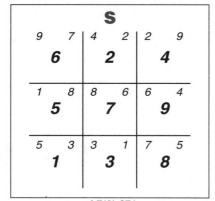

S

9 7	4 2	2 9
6	**2**	**4**
1 8	8 6	6 4
5	**7**	**9**
5 3	3 1	7 5
1	**3**	**8**

NW1-SE1

S

7 5	3 1	5 3
6	**2**	**4**
6 4	8 6	1 8
5	**7**	**9**
2 9	4 2	9 7
1	**3**	**8**

NW-SE, NW2-SE2

N1-S1

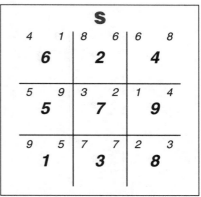

N-S, N2-S2

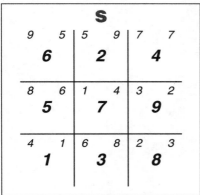

NE1-SW1

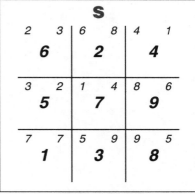

NE-SW, NE2-SW2

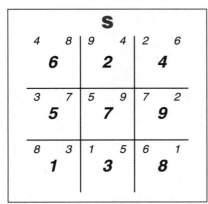

E1-W1

E-W, E2-W2

S

7 9	2 4	9 2
6	**2**	**4**
8 1	6 8	4 6
5	**7**	**9**
3 5	1 3	5 7
1	**3**	**8**

SE1-NW1

S

5 7	1 3	3 5
6	**2**	**4**
4 6	6 8	8 1
5	**7**	**9**
9 2	2 4	7 9
1	**3**	**8**

SE-NW, SE2-NW2

APPENDIX 2

How to Interpret Elemental Relationships in the Four Pillars of Destiny

1. A Metal Man

Element	People	Areas of life
Metal	Self	Colleagues, competition
Earth	Mother	Resources, support, authority
Wood	Wife, father	Wealth, money
Fire	Son	Status, pressure, power
Water	–	Intelligence, expression

2. A Wood Man

Element	People	Areas of Life
Wood	Self	Colleagues, competition
Water	Mother	Resources, support, authority
Earth	Wife, father	Wealth, money
Metal	Son	Status, pressure, power
Fire	–	Intelligence, expression

3. A Water Man

Element	People	Areas of Life
Water	Self	Colleagues, competition
Metal	Mother	Resources, support, authority
Fire	Wife, father	Wealth, money
Earth	Son	Status, pressure, power
Wood	–	Intelligence, expression

4. A Fire Man

Element	People	Areas of Life
Fire	Self	Colleagues, competition
Wood	Mother	Resources, support, authority
Metal	Wife, father	Wealth, money
Water	Son	Status, pressure, power
Earth	–	Intelligence, expression

5. An Earth Man

Element	People	Areas of Life
Earth	Self	Colleagues, competition
Fire	Mother	Resources, support, authority
Water	Wife, father	Wealth, money
Wood	Son	Status, pressure, power
Metal	–	Intelligence, expression

Note that, for a man, the elemental self-sign is defined as being the element which dominates the heavenly stem of his day pillar. The above table shows relationships for a male subject only. For a female, the differences only concern the relationship with the husband and the son. The following supplementary table shows how to read the husband and son elements in the birth data of each female self-sign:

Self	Son	Husband
Metal woman	Water	Fire
Wood woman	Fire	Metal
Water woman	Wood	Earth
Fire woman	Earth	Water
Earth woman	Metal	Wood

Since a woman gives birth to her son, his sign is the element which her self-sign gives birth to. Ancient society also considered women to be the submissive sex, so the element that conquers her self is the husband. In all other aspects the elemental relationships follow the patterns shown earlier.

The Author

Raymond Lo, also popularly known as *"Feng Shui* Lo" in Hong Kong, is a professional *feng shui* researcher and practitioner. His expertise also covers the Four Pillars of Destiny and the predictions of the *I Ching* oracle.

Having graduated with a degree in Social Sciences from the University of Hong Kong, Mr Lo's interest in *feng shui* led him to seriously study the ancient art. He subsequently learnt to explain the complicated theories of Chinese metaphysics in a concise and logical manner, using this skill to write a popular *feng shui* column in *The Hong Kong Standard* between 1988 and 1991. In this column he made several forecasts about world events, including the outbreak and the result of the Gulf War, the fall of Mr Gorbachev and Mrs Thatcher's resignation, all of which have later proved to be accurate.

Mr. Lo is also the author of *Feng Shui and Destiny* and has published three other *feng shui* titles in Chinese. He frequently contributes his knowledge of *feng shui* and the Four Pillars of Destiny to various media publications and in 1990 he made a live appearance on the popular BBC programme *Whicker's World*.